SHAME
and
GRACE

SHAME
and
GRACE

*Healing the Shame
We Don't Deserve*

Lewis B. Smedes

HarperSanFrancisco
Zondervan Publishing House
Divisions of HarperCollinsPublishers

Babette's Feast is retold by permission of Random House Publishers, Inc. From *Babette's Feast and Other Anecdotes of Destiny*. Copyright by Isak Dinesen.

SHAME AND GRACE: *Healing the Shame We Don't Deserve*. Copyright © 1993 by Lewis B. Smedes. All right reserved. Printed in the United States of America. No part of this book may be used or reproduced in any manner whatsoever without written permission except in the case of brief quotations embodied in critical articles and reviews. For information address HarperCollins Publishers, 10 East 53rd Street, New York, NY 10022.

FIRST HARPERCOLLINS EDITION CO-PUBLISHED WITH ZONDERVAN PUBLISHING HOUSE IN 1993.

ISBN 0-06-067522-5 (pbk)

An Earlier Edition of This Book Was Cataloged As Follows:

Smedes, Lewis B.
Shame and grace : healing the shame we don't deserve / Lewis B. Smedes.
   p.   cm.
Includes bibliographical references.
ISBN 0-06-067521-7 (alk. paper)
1. Shame. 2. Shame—Religious aspects—Christianity. I. Title.
BF575.S45S643 1993   92–53897
233'.4—dc20   CIP

94 95 96 97 98 ❖ HAD 10 9 8 7 6 5 4 3 2

This edition is printed on acid-free paper that meets the American National Standards Institute Z39.48 Standard.

To
David Hubbard

Contents

To the Reader

If you have a nagging feeling that you do not measure up to the person you ought to be, you are the person for whom I wrote this book.

The generic label for what you feel is *shame*. We have shame when we persistently feel that we are not acceptable, maybe unworthy, and are less than the good person we are supposed to be. Shame is a vague, undefined heaviness that presses on our spirit, dampens our gratitude for the goodness of life, and slackens the free flow of joy. Shame is a primal feeling, the kind that seeps into and discolors all our other feelings, primarily about ourself but about almost everyone and everything else in our life as well.

Shame is not necessarily a bad thing to feel. Shame can get us in touch with the most beautiful part of ourself. It can also be a warning that we are becoming the kind of person we do not really want to be. But shame is often an unhealthy feeling of unworth that is distorted, exaggerated, and utterly out of touch with our reality. Most of us carry both kinds of shame—healthy shame and unhealthy shame, that is, shame we deserve and shame we don't deserve.

The good news is that shame can be healed. I believe that the healing of our feelings of shame gets its best start with a spiritual experience—specifically, an experience of amazing grace.

Acknowledgments

Many people helped me understand shame and how to heal it, more of them than I can think of, and some of them helped me write this book about it. I want to thank them.

I have dedicated the book to David Hubbard to express to him a quarter century's accumulation of gratitude. David has been president of my school for as long as I have worked there and my gratitude for him has grown incrementally as each academic season became, for me, a blessing renewed. But at this moment, my thanks are fixed on one thing: the grace with which he curbed his passion for true scholarship and encouraged me to write the modest little books that I, from time to time, have written. Nobody else's boost could have helped as much.

I am thankful to a few good friends—John Ortberg, Elaine and Don Postema, Mary Rotzien, Carol Visser, and Doris, my wife—who read the manuscript and gave me needed criticism and encouragement. To Doris I owe added thanks for putting up with my boring self-doubts. Sam and Betty Reeves graciously invited Doris and me to their oceanside home for several days of undisturbed editing before I let go of the manuscript. My editors, John Shopp and Roland Seboldt at HarperSanFrancisco and Lyn Cryderman at Zondervan, counseled me wisely. My agent Sandra Dijkstra took my hand and broke track for me all the way, and I am indeed grateful to her. My teaching associate Ron DeVries introduced me to the works of several scholars whose research into the psychology of shame has helped me enormously: their works are included in the list at the end of this book.

I remain thankful to God for the grace which is still healing my shame.

PART ONE

The Heaviness of Shame

One

A Very Heavy Feeling

A pervasive sense of shame is the ongoing premise that one is
fundamentally bad, inadequate, defective, unworthy, or
not fully valid as a human being.

MERLE FOSSUM

shame or guilt

I felt vaguely guilty, but I could not think of anything in particular to feel guilty about. My friend Neil Warren had my number. He set his eyes in the shape of a smile when I told him this, ten or so years ago now, and said to me, "I don't think you feel guilty at all, Lew; I think that what you feel is shame."

What he said sounded like wisdom, but it took me a while to understand it. I had never had the gumption to do much bold sinning, so I was not hexed much by ghosts of former sins. But I lugged around inside of me a dead weight of not-good-enoughness. This, I sensed, was what Neil Warren meant when he said that my trouble was not guilt but shame.

About the same time, back in Muskegon, Michigan, my mother gave me my second lesson in shame. I was visiting with her at the hospital one afternoon. She was going to die in a few weeks, though only she knew it. The winter sun was setting, she was bone-tired—we had talked too long—her eyes closed now, moist at the corners, and she heaved, "Oh, Lewis, I'm so glad that the Lord forgives me all of my sins; I've been a great sinner, you know."

Great sinner? As far back as I could remember, she was on her knees scrubbing people's kitchen floors most days, up to her neck in the frets of five fussing children every evening, and, when late night fell, there she was on her knees again, in her own kitchen this time, asking the Lord for strength to do it again for one more day. When did she have time and where did she get the energy to do any great sinning?

What she was feeling about herself in those last weeks was what she had been feeling most of her life, that she was just not good enough, not a good enough mother, or a good enough Christian, or a good enough anything she could think of. But not being good enough felt to her the same as being very bad. And "great sinner" was the only way she could think of to describe the heaviness she felt.

I kept my mouth shut, but I did remember what Neil Warren had said to me, and I thought, "Mother, what makes you feel so bad about yourself is not sin but shame." That's right; my mother had a classic case of unhealthy shame. A lifelong affair with chronic not-good-enoughness. I learned my shame from her.

It saddens me still that such a triumph of a woman should have to die feeling like a wretch. Her shame was totally out of touch with her reality. She did not deserve to be stuck with so much shame.

But hold on. My mother was, no doubt about it, burdened with a shame she did not deserve, and yet in her dying and much of her living, she was wondrously serene. She was given a grace to turn her shame into peace with a life tougher than she deserved. Life with her was full of the ambiguities of shame; shame is a bad thing to experience, and yet, and yet, and yet . . .

Forget about ambiguity for a moment and let me tell you about a person with a clear case of well-deserved shame. He was a likable man; some found him charming, a successful person by manner and reputation. I'm going to call him Richard Malum. He was a master of charming evil—I mean that he knew how to get people to say yes before he asked them the question. He charmed every woman he met, charmed them while he fed them, charmed them while he used them, and charmed them when he threw them away like broken dolls.

Richard Malum charmed his customers and made them feel good about themselves while he cheated them. He gave money to strategic charities in amounts his accountant recommended, saw to it that everyone heard about his generosity, and then publicly insisted that his charity was a private matter. He climbed to the executive suite over the backs of people he stabbed to get there; getting hurt, he thought, was the price weak persons paid for competing with the strong. All the while he was doing these things, he was almost sure that he incarnated the best virtues of free enterprise. Almost sure, but not quite.

"I believed in my lies most of the time," he admitted,

> but once in a while, at about 2:00 A.M., a faint signal of the truth came over me: I was a fraud. Worse, a monster. Still, by the time I was working on my first victim of the day, I had convinced myself that I was only doing what every successful person had to do to keep ahead of the pack. I am sometimes disgusted with myself. And yet, the strange thing is that I could go back to it all tomorrow.

I was angry that this evil man should be feeling the same kind of heavy feeling about himself that my mother had felt about herself. This man's shame, I thought, is the only healthy thing left in him.

So here we are, right off the bat, with our fingers wrapped around the opposite poles of shame. It may be an unhealthy feeling that we don't deserve—my mother's feelings, for instance. It may be the only healthy feeling we have—Richard Malum's shame, for instance.

The catch is that most of us are neither as good as my mother was nor as bad as Richard Malum's was. Yet many of us feel the way both of them felt about themselves, like unworthy human beings. What we feel is called shame, and, from all reports, a great many of us feel it.

What, then, is shame, what does it feel like, and how do we know when we have it?

To begin with, shame is a very heavy feeling. It is a feeling that we do not measure up and maybe never will measure up to the sorts of persons we are meant to be. The feeling, when we are conscious of it, gives us a vague disgust with ourselves, which in turn feels like a hunk of lead on our hearts.

Almost everybody feels shame sometimes, like an invisible load that weighs our spirits down and crushes out our joy. It is a lingering sorrow. But it can also be an acute pain that stings you at the moment you are feeling best. One person described her shame to me as "a knife cutting into the heart of me just when I am feeling good about myself." But if shame is not always that sharp, it is always a heaviness as if on a long journey we were always trudging uphill or plowing through a swamp.

Shame can fall over you when a person stares at you after you've said something inane at a party, or when you think everyone is clucking at how skinny or how fat or how clumsy you are. It comes when no one else is looking at you but yourself and what you see is a phony, a coward, a bore, a failure, a dumbbell, a person whose nose is too big and whose legs are too bony, or a mother who is incompetent at mothering and, all in all, a poor dope with little hope of ever becoming an acceptable human being.

The feeling of shame is about our very *selves*—not about some bad thing we *did* or *said* but about what we *are*. It tells us that we *are* unworthy. Totally. It is not as if a few seams in the garment of our selves need stitching; the whole fabric is frayed. We feel that we *are* unacceptable. And to feel that is a life-wearying heaviness. Shame-burdened people are the sort whom Jesus had in mind when he invited the "weary and heavy laden" to trade their heaviness for his lightness.

Here are some shame-toned feelings that people have expressed to me and that I have felt from time to time. You may want to ask yourself whether they express feelings that you have had.

> I sometimes feel as if I am a fake.
>
> I feel that if people who admire me really knew me they might have contempt for me.
>
> I feel inadequate; I seldom feel as if I am up to what is expected of me.
>
> When I look inside of myself, I seldom feel any joy at what I am.
>
> I feel inferior to the really good people that I know.
>
> I feel as if God must be disgusted with me.

Paul's books

I feel flawed inside, blemished somehow, dirty sometimes.

I feel as if I just cannot measure up to what I ought to be.

I feel as if I will never be acceptable.

If you persistently feel the sort of feelings expressed in these sentences, you are feeling shame.

The tough question is whether it is always a bad thing to feel shame. Charlie Chaplin, the immortal comic, now—in *The Lamplighter*—a sad old man, gave a deep sigh and murmured, "The trouble with the whole world is that we despise ourselves." Psychologists today tend to agree with Charlie Chaplin.

Gershen Kaufman, whose research into shame helped break the trail, says that "shame is without parallel—a sickness of the soul." Sometimes it is, but then again, sometimes shame may be our hope for health. Again, Kaufman says that shame is a "violation [of] . . . our essential dignity." Sometimes it is. However, shame is sometimes our last contact with what is most human and dignified about us. Besides, if shame makes us feel like worms, it may also be that some of us are worms.

Whether healthy or unhealthy, true or false, shame is always a heavy feeling of being an unacceptable person, a feeling that, one way or the other, needs healing.

To get a clearer picture of our own feeling, it will help if we compare it to a few other feelings, heavy the way shame is heavy, feelings that feel something like shame and yet not the same. This we will do in the next chapter.

Two

Shame's Close Relations

Feelings are mushy, difficult, non-palpable, slippery things . . .
difficult to quantify, difficult to communicate, difficult even
to distinguish within ourselves one from the other.

WILLARD GAYLIN

Feelings flow into and out of each other like the sounds of four in-
struments in a string quartet; each produces its own authentic tones,
yet the sounds of violins and viola and cello flow so fluidly into each
other that we do not even try to hear their separate sounds. So it is
with shame and other similar feelings. They flow into and out of each
other, and it sometimes becomes hard to tell one feeling from the
other.

What shall we call the feeling we have today? Are we feeling guilty,
embarrassed, discouraged, depressed, frustrated, or just plain tired?
Or are we feeling shame? Our feelings are close relatives. But they are
as different from each other as first cousins can be. Let us look a bit
closer at some of the differences.

Feeling Guilt and Feeling Shame

The difference between guilt and shame is very clear—in theory. We
feel guilty for what we *do*. We feel shame for what we *are*. A person
feels guilt because he *did* something wrong. A person feels shame because he *is* something wrong. We may feel guilty because we lied to

our mother. We may feel shame because we are not the persons our mother wanted us to be.

In reality, the feelings of guilt and shame overlap. We do feel guilty for what we do, but we can also feel shame because of something we do. A person may feel guilty for telling a lie to his wife and feel shame for being the sort of person who would do such a thing.

I must tell you one story to illustrate the point. It is about two splendid writers whose work I admire. One of them was a young Jewish journalist, and the other was an elderly Christian novelist. The journalist later became one of the most honored writers of our time, and the novelist was at that time one of the most acclaimed writers in France. Their names are Elie Wiesel and François Mauriac.

When he was a boy Wiesel had been freighted with his parents to a concentration camp. Both of his parents had been killed; he had survived. The war had been over a while and Wiesel was working for a Yiddish newspaper in Paris. Though he had become a journalist, he had made a vow never to write a single word about his experience. The suffering of the Holocaust, he felt, was so awesome that telling of it in human words could only profane its sacred horror.

In Paris, Wiesel learned to idolize François Mauriac. But one thing about the great writer annoyed him. Mauriac was given to talking a lot about Jesus, and Wiesel thought he overdid it. One evening, when the young journalist was a guest at Mauriac's apartment and Mauriac had been going on about Jesus again, Wiesel had his fill of it.

He blurted out, "Mr. Mauriac, you are forever talking about the suffering of Jesus, but I can tell you that I have with my own eyes seen little Jewish children suffer more than Jesus suffered." There, he had said it, spat it in the face of this great man, and he was crushed by a wave of shame. "What sort of person would do such a thing?"

Wiesel stood on his feet, hung his head, and made for the door. As he was about to go outside, Mauriac asked him please to wait a moment. The aging author walked over to Wiesel, put a hand on his shoulder, and said, "Mr. Wiesel, I do believe that it is a mistake for you not to write about the Holocaust."

Wiesel had *done* something and felt ashamed of him*self* for doing it. Never mind now that he had not done anything that made him guilty of breaking some moral law; noble hearts feel deep shame for acts that literalists hardly notice. The point is that what Wiesel *did* to the revered writer made him feel not so much guilty as ashamed.

Enough then to show that feelings of guilt and feelings of shame are fluid feelings that never stay in their own place quite the way our labels want them to. Still, the distinction helps, and I will go along with it as best I can: *guilt* will be mostly about things we have done and shame mostly about what we *are*.

(By the way, Wiesel did write about his experience as a child in the Holocaust; he wrote it in Yiddish while he was living in South America. Mauriac got hold of the Yiddish manuscript, saw personally to its translation, and arranged on his own to have it published in French. In English it has the title *Night* and is doubtless the most gripping of all the books about the Holocaust.)

Feeling Embarrassed and Feeling Shame

We feel properly embarrassed when we are caught doing something that makes us look inept, knuckleheaded, or inappropriate. Maybe the difference is this: we feel embarrassed because we *look* bad, and we feel shame because we think we *are* bad. When we are embarrassed, we feel socially foolish. When we are shamed, we feel morally unworthy.

A couple of years ago Doris and I went to a snug, round theater called the Mark Taper Forum at the Music Center in Los Angeles to see a performance of Shakespeare's *Julius Caesar* in a modern setting. It was a matinee performance, starting at precisely 2:30 in the afternoon. It so happened that at 2:30 on that particular afternoon, there were exactly two minutes left to play in the deciding game of the semifinals in the NBA championship basketball playoffs. My team, the Los Angeles Lakers, was playing the Portland Trail Blazers, and the score was tied when the curtain went up.

Looking ahead to this possibility, I smuggled a Walkman inside the theater, put on the earphones, and listened to the staccato play-by-play of Chick Hearn, the Lakers' broadcaster, while I watched the first scene of the tragedy of Julius Caesar unfold.

My wife glanced at me; I thought she was asking me to tell her the score of the basketball game. I intended to whisper it for only her ears to hear, but the crowd at the basketball game was yelling and screaming in my earphones and I had to make myself heard above the racket, which I did. I yelled, "Eighteen seconds to go; Lakers down by a point!"

Fifteen rows ahead of me, startled patrons turned around, shocked. Mark Antony missed a cue.

At intermission time I needed to find a bathroom, and I decided to make my move out into the lobby. A tike of a woman half my size and more than my age was waiting for me; she blocked my path and hissed that I ought to be ashamed of myself. I told her I was sorry and that it was an accident. No excuse; she just hoped to God my shameful behavior was a momentary lapse and not a way of life and that I ought to be ashamed and stand up and apologize to the cast. People standing around in the lobby listened to her and watched me; they were on her side.

For three days, I felt like a fatally flawed person standing shamed before the harsh judgment of my cultured superiors. But was it shame? Or acute chagrin? For a little while, I suffered shame for being an inferior human being, and then, brought back to sanity, I felt embarrassment at being a nincompoop at the theater.

Feeling Discouraged and Feeling Shame

Once, after a tough day on the scaffolding, painting his immense masterpiece of the creation of the world on the ceiling of the Sistine Chapel, Michelangelo wrote a sonnet to his pain. The final line in the sonnet was:

I am not a painter.

Michelangelo, greatest of all artists, not a painter? Terribly discouraging. But no shame. The next morning, he was on the scaffold again, brushes in his hands and brushes in his teeth, painting his vision of the Maker of the universe reaching out his life-channeling arm to ignite his noblest creation with the light of his life.

We all get tired sometimes. The load gets heavy, and we feel as if we cannot do what we need to do or make it to where we need to go.

Maxey Dean Filer, of Compton, California, was sure that he was born to be a lawyer, but the bar exams in California are tough. He took the exam forty-seven times and failed every time. Maxey had recently turned sixty, and thirty-seven years of failing left him feeling pretty sure that he was going to die and never get to be what he was born to be. Terribly discouraged, Maxey Filer was never ashamed. He took the exam again one more time, took it for the forty-eighth time. He passed.

When I feel discouraged, I feel for a while that I am not up to *doing* the *job* I feel I need to do. When I feel shame, I have a chronic hunch that I am not up to *being* the *person* I need to be.

Being Depressed and Feeling Shame

We use the word *depression* to describe everything from the blues of a rainy Monday to the madness of acute deprivation of one's very self.

I know from experience that a shame-prone person is also depression-prone. While my shame was gradually seducing me into depression, the heaviness did not abruptly turn into a depression. It just kept getting heavier. Once into depression, my feeling became much, much heavier, so much so that it became something qualitatively different from shame. No one can tell in advance when one may cross that line.

William Styron described his own descent into the madness of depression in his book *Darkness Invisible*. He tells us that two experiences dominated him. One was the experience of loss. The other was the experience of hopelessness.

"Loss," he says, "in all of its manifestations is the touchstone of depression. . . . I felt loss at every hand. The loss of self-esteem is a celebrated symptom, and my own sense of self had all but disappeared," and finally, nearing the penultimate depths of depression, "the acute sense of . . . life slipping away at accelerated speed." Then came hopelessness: "It is hopelessness even more than pain that crushes the soul. . . . My brain . . . had become less an organ of thought than an instrument registering . . . varying degrees of its own suffering . . . and what makes the condition so intolerable is the foreknowledge that no remedy will come—not in a day, an hour, a month, or a minute."

The simplest, and an unscientific, way to mark the difference between shame and the depression that Styron experienced is that depression is worse, deeper, and more debilitating than shame.

Feeling Frustrated and Feeling Shame

Tony Gwynn of the San Diego Padres, an artist with a baseball bat in his hands, feels frustrated when he ends the season with a .330 batting average. It is good enough to be the best in the major leagues. But to a perfectionist like Gwynn, a .330 batting average means that he failed to get a hit almost two out of every three times at bat.

The fact is that Tony Gwynn has limits that frustrate him. His limits are set for him by the realities of the game he plays. He has to hit a small round ball that somebody throws at him on an unpredictable trajectory from sixty feet and six inches away, sometimes at ninety miles an hour. Once it leaves the pitcher's fingers, a ball shot to him at that speed takes .4167 second to reach the plate. And Gwynn is never sure what crazy curves and dips the ball will take before it arrives. So he is limited by the pitcher.

Another limit is the fact that he has to hit the small round ball with a round piece of wood. Once he decides to swing, he has about two-tenths of a second to get his arms to bring the bat to the ball. Then, if he makes contact, he hits the ball toward nine fielders who seldom drop it.

In short, Gwynn faces limits that prevent anyone who does not have rare talent and intense dedication from ever getting a single hit. Gwynn gets more than his share. But he still feels frustrated by these limits because he wants to get a hit every time he tries.

We are destined to feel frustrated at times because we have the power to imagine that we can defy our limits. In our imagination, we may enjoy the illusion that we have no limits, but we reach them sooner or later, and when we do, we chafe. To be frustrated by our limits is our destiny and our discomfort; it is our challenge to reach beyond them. But it is our glory, not our shame.

Feelings are not precise, nor are they firm. They are fuzzy and slippery and hard to get our hands on. There is usually no great loss if we do not get the right labels attached to our feelings. However, as we seek healing for our shame, we should not try to heal what does not need healing. It is important to look for the differences between what needs healing and what does not.

Three

Leading Candidates for Shame

He was not born to shame; upon his brow shame is ashamed to sit.
WILLIAM SHAKESPEARE

Many good people develop a diminished immunity to shame, especially to shame they do not deserve to feel. It is not as if they have more to be ashamed of than your run-of-the-mill sinner. They tend, in fact, to be unusually conscientious people.

It is not hard to spot our candidates. I will try to describe some of them. You can decide whether you recognize at least a part of yourself in them.

Guilt Spreaders

Guilt overflow the banks of action and flood our being with shame. White water from a flowing river becomes a fetid swamp once it settles into the valley. So guilt becomes a stagnant shame after it has flowed from one thing we did over all that we are.

The shame equation is this: one wrong act equals one bad person.

There was once in the city of Karpov, it is said, a gifted piano player named Lech Koplenski who, because he had no connections in the concert world, played the piano every night at a popular cabaret. Chenska Wolenka was an attractive woman who loved Lech with a selfless devotion to his dream of becoming a concert pianist.

A producer of concerts often came to the cabaret, and Chenska struck up a friendship with him so that she could bring Lech to his attention.

The producer of concerts made Chenska a proposition. If she would make love with him, he would see to it that Lech got his chance on the concert stage. She agreed, and in his bed she made good on her bargain. The producer made good on his as well. Lech did indeed play the piano on the concert stage.

Lech went off on concert tours, became a star, and did not come back to the cabaret. All that Chenska had left over was a deep shame of herself. One early morning in May she jumped from her apartment window to her death in a Karpov alley. Taped to her mirror was this sentence:

I am filth.

I did, therefore I am; this is the fatal equation.

Let such people tell one lie, and in the twinkling of an eye, they are liars. They commit one act of infidelity, and they are therewith adulterers. They go to a party, talk too much, tell a story to the left of good taste, are reminded of it on the way home, and sink into a funky shame for being half-witted fools. This makes about the same sense as saying that if you pound a nail in a piece of wood you become a carpenter.

The Overly Responsible

Overly responsible people feel as if they, not God, have the whole world in their hands. Everything that goes badly in the lives of people around them is somehow their responsibility. If they cannot fix it, they must be inadequate and unworthy.

Not long ago, I had to tell a student named Helena that her best friend back home had taken her own life. I invited Helena to tell me about her friend and about herself. She told me that her friend was unusually sensitive to the suffering of the world's poor people. In some unchartered moral sense she was accountable for starving children in Ethiopia, oppressed blacks in South Africa, massacred citizens in Cambodia, all the homeless men and women in the cities of the United States, and the happiness of her own family to boot.

The world was wracked in pain; its agony lay on her heart. She was ashamed that she could do so little to heal its wounds. It all became too heavy for her, and she could not bear her shame anymore. She died of chronic too-muchness.

After telling me about her friend, Helena began to accuse herself. If she had stayed where she was, gone to school in her hometown, and stuck with her friend, maybe she could have saved her friend's life. I knew exactly what she was feeling. Some of us feel doomed, like Atlas, to bear the whole world on our backs.

A friend of mine went up one night to the hills behind my house and put a bullet in his head. He was a physician by trade, and a reformer by inclination. To me he was simply the most generous person I had ever known, but he thought he was responsible for repairing an irreparable world.

I recalled that he had not been in touch with me for a few months. If I had called him, I might have said something that would have made him change his mind. What sort of friend was I? In the dead of night, a month or so after he killed himself, a menacing message came into my head. A dream? I wasn't sure.

"He was a far, far better person than I; how can I deserve to live if he did not?"

I sat up in bed. I was seized by a feeling that I owed it to my friend to kill myself. I tried to think of someone I could call up at that hour to get permission not to commit suicide. I did not have the courage to make the call. But the life force from God overcame the death force of my shame, and I lived.

People who cannot believe that only God has the whole world in his hands are candidates for shame they do not deserve.

Obsessive Moralizers

Some people see life totally in moral colors, as if everything we do has to be either right or wrong. Nothing may ever be only fun or only delicious or only exciting. We may never simply taste life; we must always measure it, weigh it, evaluate it to see whether it is morally sound.

The result is that these people feel vaguely immoral when they do anything slightly outlandish. They feel the same when they violate custom as they do when they violate conscience, the same when they act the buffoon as when they act the liar. Every offbeat bit of silliness is morally serious; every goof becomes a demonstration of moral deficiency. Their cool heads tell them that some things are just for the fun of it, but their feelings will not listen.

Compulsive Comparers

Some people feel a shame they do not deserve because they are forever comparing themselves with successful people. Every time their friends succeed, they feel like failures. Everybody else's sun darkens their day.

Ed Dekker, our neighbor once removed, wore clean white overalls over a clean white shirt whenever he puttered around his clean white house. He drove around western Michigan in his Buick coupe selling Dutch Boy White Lead paint, which he spread on his own white house every other year.

For breakfast, Ed ate grapefruit with a strawberry nested in the center and honey poured over the top. But the clearest token of his class was a white birdhouse he built for swarms of purple martins sailing like tiny gulls in the Michigan sky. The birdhouse had eight round holes on each of its four sides opening to the guest rooms inside. It was perched on a white pillar thirty feet high. Each October, after the martins emigrated, the men of the neighborhood gathered to ease the house down from its pillar so that Ed Dekker could put a new coat of Dutch Boy White Lead on it.

Ed trained his own bird dogs, English setters, thoroughbreds they were. Wintertimes, in his clean white basement, he carved butts for his shotguns from fine teak that he ordered out of a gentleman hunter's catalogue. He kept sharp by shooting at clay pigeons— which were black bowls with flat bottoms—at the gun club during the off season. Sometimes he took me along to spring the pigeons from a contraption that spun them a couple of hundred yards into the air. At the apex of their flight, Ed Dekker shattered them with his dandy gun. When he had downed his limit, he would let me ride home in his rumble seat.

At our house, Ed Dekker was a terror. My mother would think of inviting Franklin Delano Roosevelt over for a cup of coffee sooner than she would have asked Ed Dekker. His fussiness was a reminder of our messiness, his elegance of our commonness, his pride of our shame.

People with Ed Dekkers in their heads are prone to shame. Anyone else's success is the mirror of their failure. Anyone else's beauty is the reflection in which they see their own plainness. Anyone else's talent is their ineptitude. They suffer from compulsive comparisons, and this makes them candidates for undeserved shame.

Approval Addicts

Some people cannot approve of themselves unless they know for sure that other people approve of them—like them, admire them, say nice things about them behind their backs, and let them know that they are acceptable. Low on ego strength, they suck their self-esteem from others.

Such people never get enough. A compliment today must be applause tomorrow, and applause tomorrow has to be a standing ovation the next day. Like any addict, they need to keep increasing the dose.

So these people turn their lives into a run for somebody's approval. Whose? Anybody's. A professor's approval. An audience's approval. Most of all, the approval of the two people who nagged them from the beginning to make something of themselves and become a person Mother and Dad and God could approve of.

Their parents are stand-ins for God, and they are often hard put to keep the two distinct in their own hopes and fears. If Dad or Mom cannot approve of them, it feels as if God is disapproving, and so the threat of father's or mother's disapproval becomes a shadow of shame over the lives of the children.

The Never Deserving

While I was a graduate student in Amsterdam, a vicious North Sea storm collided with a high tide one February night and broke the dykes. A few minutes after the dykes broke, the low farmlands of the province of Zeeland were covered with the waters of the deep. Houses floated on the ocean top as villages became the ocean's floor.

Nature's preference for life pushed some of the people to their roofs. But when small boats finally came by to pick the people off, they refused to leave, saying, "No, no, this is God's judgment; if the Lord does not consider us deserving, we will not interfere with his judgment." Some very good farmers of the province of Zeeland perished because of a shame they did not deserve.

Shame can happen to more sophisticated people, too. A professional woman I know who has the highest academic credentials available and is a first-class person besides cannot make herself feel that she deserves the tidbits of luxury that now and then sneak into her life. If she is on a vacation and finds herself in a class A hotel, she is miserable. If the service were horrid, the food wretched, and the beds lumpy, she might feel more deserving of what she had. But if everything is superb, she cannot enjoy it.

Another woman I know, a competent woman, a comer in her business, is driven to demeaning encounters with dependent men who cannot cope on their own. Why? Why must she forever rescue losers? Why can she not find a good man and love him as her equal? Ask her:

I don't feel that I deserve a good man.

People who cannot enjoy the good gifts of life because they feel that they do not deserve those gifts really mean that they are not worthy of them. Being deserving and being worthy are not the same. Any healthy person knows that many of the good things in life are sheer gifts; she knows she did not earn them and, in that sense, does not deserve them but gratefully accepts them. The hitch comes when we leap from feeling undeserving to feeling unworthy. This is the feeling that makes a person ripe for shame.

People Condemned by Bad Memories

It is rumored that a certain psychologist in one of the Iron Curtain countries during the days of Joseph Stalin had an uncanny way of getting innocent people to confess to just about any crime against the state that Stalin decided to accuse them of. This psychologist could get them to confess to anything at all, even things they would never have dreamed of doing. Their confessions got them a cell in one of Stalin's gulags.

A visitor from the West asked the psychologist for the secret of his success.

"I work on the Mongolian peasant hypothesis."

"Mongolian peasant?"

"Yes, the secret of my success is my belief that everyone has a Mongolian peasant."

"Tell me what you mean."

The psychologist told this story:

A nobody of a man, shabby and ill at ease, is brought into a large office that clearly belongs to an important person. Everything there smacks of authority: dark mahogany walls; a huge oak desk, uncluttered, a small flag on one corner of it; behind it, in a high leather chair, an erect, gray-haired man wearing a general's uniform with rows of medals on his chest. The general speaks:

"I have a million rubles in my desk drawer. Here, take a look. They are all yours."

"Mine?"

"On one condition."

"What condition?"

"You must press this small red button on my desk."

"What happens when I press the button?"

"An old man in Mongolia drops dead."

"He dies?"

"He dies at once, no pain."

"What for? What has he done?"

"That is not your business. Trust me. It is for the good of the people. All you need to know is that the moment you press the button, the peasant dies. And you get a million rubles."

The man presses the button. He takes the money and goes home to live with the memory that to get some money he has killed a stranger who did him no harm. He would not have done it for a few rubles, of course. Not even for a thousand, not for ten thousand. But a million? Who could refuse?

The man knows in his heart that the amount of money made no difference. He killed an innocent stranger to get it. After five years, he commits suicide. The million rubles are stuffed in a sack under his bed; the state takes them back the day of his funeral.

Everybody, according to the psychologist, has a Mongolian peasant in his life. Everyone has once harmed another person for his own advantage. The psychologist digs around in the memory until he finds the peasant. Once he has it, he dangles it in front of the accused person until that person is writhing in shame for being such a wretched human being. He will confess to anything in order to atone for his shame.

When I was sixteen, I had a job washing dishes and dispensing drinks at a ritzy soda fountain and coffee shop in Muskegon, Michigan, across the street from the Michigan Theater, the best picture show in town. A customer would walk up and take a seat on a high stool in front of a genuine marble bar and order herself a Coca Cola. I would serve it to her in a slim-bottomed, round-bosomed drinking glass that had the name Coca Cola etched on its side. For this the customer would pay a nickel. The candy shop also had booths where Muskegon's better class would eat hot-fudge sundaes and drink hot chocolate before heading home after the show.

One night two young black people, a man and a woman, walked in and sat down in one of the booths. Gus Ballas, who owned the shop, was there; I watched him as the couple walked in. He gave a quick shake of his head to the waitresses.

The white patrons drifted in, sat down in the booths; waitresses came to bring them their hot-fudge sundaes and their cups of hot chocolate, which they ate and slurped while they flirted and gabbed about the moving picture they had seen. As soon as they finished, other patrons grabbed the empty seats and played out the same script.

The black couple sat through two sittings. Nobody looked at them—except me; I glanced at them out of the corner of my eye.

They did not speak to each other or even look at each other. They did not signal to a waitress or ask to speak to the manager. They just sat there. Finally, the man signaled to his friend, and they walked out together.

They had to pass by the soda fountain where I was standing. I wanted to tell them that I was sorry. I wanted to throw down my apron and tell Gus Ballas to take his job and shove it. But I needed the job more than I wanted my honor. I poured another Coca Cola.

Now and then I remember what happened. It does not matter that nobody had heard about civil rights in Muskegon, Michigan, when I was sixteen or that I needed the job. I have my own Mongolian peasant and he shames me.

Those Who Dwell in the Shadows of Their Fathers

A child at Hartford Street Christian School was a somebody if his dad was a somebody, and a dad was a somebody if he did the right sort of work. It was natural for Mrs. Heethuis, my fourth-grade teacher, to begin the new schoolyear with a new class by asking each pupil to tell the rest of the class what sort of work his or her dad did.

Mrs. Heethuis began with Martha Aardsma, who sat in the front seat in the row next to the windows. The teacher would work back and then forward down the next row and back again and so on until she knew where each child stood. Since my last name began with the letter *S*, I sat at a desk halfway down the last row.

The call rolled up and down the aisles until it landed on me.

"What does you father do, Lewis?"

"Nothing."

"Nothing? Surely your father does something."

"He doesn't do anything."

"Doesn't do anything? Was he laid off?"

"No."

"What then?"

"He's dead."

Why should a boy feel shame to say that his father is dead?

I was walking down the street in Amsterdam one wet day and felt a need to stop at one of the city's handy sidewalk latrines. A male in distress could locate such a comfort station every few blocks in the center of town. (Women were not so thoughtfully accommodated.) The latrine was surrounded by a circular metal screen six feet high, high enough to hide the head; its bottom side began a foot off the ground so that a man's shoes and pant cuffs signaled, as it did to me on this occasion, that somebody was inside.

A man came out of the latrine carrying a bucket, a mop, and a bottle of soap—the tools of his trade. He walked over to his bicycle, put each tool in its proper bracket, and pedaled off. I suppose this man may have spent eight hours a day mopping up one latrine after another. Five days a week. Fifty weeks a year. For thirty years. This is what a man's life can come to: 277,500 clean sidewalk latrines, assuming he managed thirty-seven per day.

As I watched the man bike off in dignity, I imagined his young son, a fifth-grader as I was in Mrs. Heethuis's class, waiting his turn while the kids of his class reported on their fathers' vocations.

"My father is a cleaner of the latrines."

I hoped he would not feel the shame I felt in Mrs. Heethuis's roll call.

People Who Feel Condemned by Their Dreams

Some people cannot separate themselves from their dreams. They feel as if they are in reality what they do in their dreams. Therefore, when they dream that they do bad things, they wake up feeling ashamed of themselves for the bad things they did in their dream world.

Ten years ago I had a series of six dreams in which I tried to rescue a small dog that got into all kinds of trouble. Every Wednesday night, I had a new dream about the dog.

The dreams began on the white sand beach of Lake Michigan, where we lit driftwood fires and roasted wieners in my college days. It was turning dark, and I was walking alone on the beach. I came to a hole someone had dug in the sand; it was about four feet across and about eight feet deep. On the bottom was a bed of hot charcoal. A medium-sized, nondescript dog lay helpless on the burning coals.

The dog twisted its body some but did not yelp or seem to be in terrible agony. I watched and was horrified, but I could not reach him.

Could not? Or would not? I was not sure.

When I woke up, I was overwhelmed with shame. As I recalled the dream, I felt that if I had truly wanted to help the dog, I could have done something, though I didn't know what. I tried to persuade myself that I was not responsible for what I dreamed about. But I was not sure.

In the next-to-the-last dream, I was in Grand Rapids, Michigan, on a Sunday morning in the dead of winter. I was riding a bike through three or four feet of snow when I came on the dog, lying bleeding in the street. He had been struck by a car. I picked up the dog, put him in the wire basket attached to the handlebars of my bike, and set out to look for a veterinarian who might be doing business early on a Sunday morning in the wintertime. I pedaled through high drifts of snow until at last I found an animal doctor in his office. He looked at the dog and told me that he would need to operate. I asked him how much it would cost.

The moment I asked the doctor what his price would be, I woke up with a fierce shame. How could I have been so tight, so mean as to think about money when the dog's life may have been at stake? Must I be forever a miserable tightwad? For shame.

So much for the candidates for undeserved shame. If you recognize yourself as one of them, you may be more shame-prone than you need to be.

PART TWO

The Varieties of Shame

Four

Healthy Shame:
A Voice from Our True Self

The feeling of shame is a fact which absolutely distinguishes
[us] from lower nature.

VLADIMIR SOLOVIEV

There is a nice irony in shame: our feelings of inferiority are a sure sign of our superiority, and our feelings of unworthiness testify to our great worth. Only a very noble being can feel shame. The reason is simple: a creature meant to be a little less than God is likely to feel a deep dissatisfaction with herself if she falls a notch below the splendid human being she is meant to be. If we never feel shame, we may have lost contact with the person we most truly are. If we can still feel the pain, it is because we are healthy enough to feel uncomfortable with being less than we ought to be and less than we want to be. This is healthy shame.

Some psychologists seem to assume that all bad feelings we have about ourselves are unhealthy. I believe that they are mistaken. They work on the assumption that our *feelings* of unworthiness are our basic problem rather than the symptom of a still deeper problem. To this I say: not so fast. If we feel like flawed persons, it may be because we are in fact flawed. Our shame may be a painful signal that we are failing to be the persons we are meant to be and may therefore be the first hope of healing. Let us at least explore the possibility that a certain kind of shame may be good for us.

Shame May Be a Call from Our True Selves

"Be not ashamed of feeling shame or scornful of its purpose," Willard Gaylin wrote in his book *Feelings*. He added, "These emotions—guilt and shame—guide us to our better selves." It is good to know that we have a better self to be called back to, and it is good to know that our shame keeps us in touch with that better self. A healthy sense of shame is perhaps the surest sign of our divine origin and our human dignity. When we feel this sense of shame, we are feeling a nudge from our true selves.

Where is this so-called true self? Is it hiding somewhere inside of us, like a forgotten ghost who haunts us with memories of the self we used to be? What is it like? How do we know it when we see it?

Our true self is like the design for a building still under construction or the original design for a building that needs restoring. It is stamped in the depths of us like a template for the selves we are meant to be and yet are failing to be.

Christians recognize the pattern of their true selves in the story of Jesus. We may also recognize it when we see it in the lives of our heroes and saints. We feel it in the pressure we get from our own conscience when it works right. We know it by a deep intuition we have of the better person we would be if we truly were all we could be.

Our actual self—the self we are from day to day—never quite matches the template of our true self. In fact, the gap between our true self and our actual self is what creates our healthy feelings of shame. So, before I talk about our true self, I had better explain what I mean by our actual self.

Our actual self exists on two levels.

Our self on the upper level is the self we are more or less in charge of. It is the inner self we are in the thoughts we think and feelings we feel. It is the outer self we are in our families and with our friends and in our neighborhoods and at our jobs, the self we are in all the roles we play. It is the self we create out of our commitments to people, the self that people count on to be just about the same person today that we were yesterday.

The lower level self is the self we are not much in charge of. It is the self of impulses we do not choose to have and urges that often control us. It is the hidden self, the self of our shadows, of our subconscious, the self of the ogres and demons that tease and cavort in the cellars of our souls, the self that speaks to us in the strange dreams we dream. It is a puzzling, frightening self, too sneaky, too elusive for us to grasp, but still a part of our actual selves as surely as its darker side is part of the moon.

Shame comes on us when our actual self, on either level, is in conflict with the true self we were meant to be. What, then, do we mean by our true self? Any image of the true self is blended from many ingredients. I will run through a few of them. You can decide for yourself whether they actually match at least parts of your own image of the truest and best you—the self that in your best moments you want to be.

First, your true self is a grateful person. You feel the gladness that comes when you sense that every breath, every heartbeat, every good feeling, every touch of another person's friendly flesh on yours, and every loving relationship another person offers you are all wonderful gifts to you. They are all God's gifts that you accept and relish and enjoy, and accepting them makes you feel wondrously fortunate and blessed.

Second, your true self is an integrated whole. Your life holds together; you are one. You are the same person in secret that you are in public, you have the courage to face unpleasant realities without disguising them, you have a natural bent for accepting and telling the truth even when you pay a price for telling it; and you try to keep your promises even when it costs you some inconvenience and sacrifice. In short, you are a person of integrity.

Third, your true self is tuned to what is really going on around you—and in you. You listen to the voices, you look at the sights, and you smell the scents of reality around you. You see connections, the links between things, how one thing relates to another. You see the differences between things; you can tell the difference, for instance, between what is important and what can wait until tomorrow. You see things in yourself you are proud of, and you admit to things you feel ashamed of. In short, you are a discerning person.

Fourth, your true self is the conductor of your private inner orchestra. You manage your passions. You are not afraid to get angry, but you do not lose control of your temper. You have a powerful capacity for pleasure, but you are not addicted. You can let yourself go, but you are not a slave of your own impulses or other people's seductions. You are the sort of person whom other people can count on because you are in charge of your life.

Fifth, your true self has a freedom to love with passion. Your love desires all that your loved one can give you, but your love is also a strong desire to give her all she needs from you. Your love is strong enough to go on loving even when the fire of passion dies down. You make people better and freer persons for having been loved by you. Your true self is a true lover.

There they are, just for starters, five ingredients of our true self. Do you not recognize in them at least parts of the self you were meant to be? And want to be? But the self you never quite are? Is it not clear that the shame you sometimes feel is a gift to you precisely because it calls you back to your better self?

Shame is a flame from the glowing ember of our original fire. The ember still burns at the core of our lives, still shines in our memories, still glimmers in our hopes, and still invites us to be one with her again.

How does our true self get its message to us? In many ways. Some of us get it straight from our conscience. Some of us get it from the stories of those who went before us. Some of us learn it from what wise and profound minds have taught us. All of us get it because the divine Spirit prods and pushes, nudges and shoves us with intimations of the better self we were created to be.

Shame May Be a Symptom of Something Going Wrong

Shame, we are told, is the painful feeling of being a flawed human being. Well, what if, in fact, we *are* flawed human beings? All of us. Cracked vessels. Wheels out of alignment. The heart of us slightly off center. What if none of us is quite a match for the self we could be?

Given the horrors that some members of our species consistently inflict on others, why should we blame our shame? Why should we not be thankful that we still have the power to feel it? Given the crabbed side of my own spirit, my irresistible urge to seek my own interests at the cost of others, my comfort in the teeth of other people's suffering, my niggardly envy of other people's success, and given my urges to smash the nose of any driver who cuts in front of me, given such flaws, am I not more in tune with reality if I accept my shame as the cost of failing to be the self I ought to be, the self I am meant to be, and the self I really want to be? This is healthy shame, and we are closest to health when we let ourselves feel the pain of it and be led by the pain to do something about it.

If I never feel shame, I have become either totally divine or totally corrupt—and my best intuitions tell me I am neither.

Shame Protects Us from Our Falseness

Our shame may be our best defense against our folly. When it comes down to it, most people do the right thing because they would be ashamed of themselves if they did the wrong thing. It is not the fear of breaking the Ten Commandments or the threat of punishment that keeps them true to themselves. More often than not, they avoid the cheap, the mean, and the fake because they do not want to feel ashamed of themselves.

There is a fascinating character by the name of Tarrou in Albert Camus's novel *The Plague.* He has been helping Dr. Rieux take care of all the dying people in the plague-struck town of Oran. What the epidemic of plague taught him was, as he put it, that "each of us has the Plague within him; no one, no one on earth is free from it."

Tarrou recalls one day how he watched a young man of thirty or so who was on trial for murder. The young man—maybe guilty, but probably innocent—was convicted and sentenced to die. Tarrou never forgot the shame he felt on hearing a human being condemned to die.

> For many years, I've been ashamed, mortally ashamed, of having been, even with the best of intentions, even at many removes, a murderer in my turn. . . . Yes, I've been ashamed ever since. So that is why I resolved to have no truck with anything which, directly or indirectly, for good reasons or for bad, brings death to anyone or justifies others' putting him to death.

Tarrou's shame pushed him to live in risky ways that gave others a better chance to live. Not the best of all reasons for living nobly, but a real one for all that and one that works fairly well for most of us.

Shame Is a Chance to Understand Ourselves

Shame has no intelligence; it does not reason with us. It is a feeling. However, whenever we feel shame, it sets us at a cross-road. We have a choice: do we rush to get relief, or do we first ask what causes the pain?

To ask why we are feeling the sting of shame is a step into self-understanding. When we probe our shame, we may discover a great deal about ourselves that is worth knowing. What we find out about ourselves may disappoint us deeply. It may also make us feel grateful for the good qualities we had not dared give ourselves credit for before. But whatever there is for us to discover inside ourselves, shame may be the push we need to make us look and see.

As we bore through the crust of feelings we do not understand, we may also discover deep pools of shame that somebody caused us before we knew what was happening. We may feel for the first time the full sting of a shame that we do not deserve, a shame someone injected into us by treating us as if we were a shameful child. Waves of sadness may pour out into our consciousness, our heart may be breaking, and only when we see where our shame came from will we know why it feels so heavy and why we do not deserve to feel it at all.

Five

Unhealthy Shame:
A Voice from Our False Self

*My life has been spent in vain and idle aspirations, and in
ceaseless rejected prayers that something beneficial
should be the result of my existence.*

JOHN QUINCY ADAMS

Ambassador to Holland, Ambassador to Great Britain, Ambassador to Russia,
Secretary of State, Senator, and President of the United States

Shame can be like a signal from a drunken signalman who warns of
a train that is not coming. The pain of this shame is not a signal of
something wrong in us that needs to be made right. Our shame is
what is wrong with us. It is a false shame because the feeling has no
basis in reality. It is unhealthy shame because it saps our creative
powers and kills our joy. It is a shame we do not deserve because we
are not as bad as our feelings tell us we are. Undeserved shame is a
good gift gone bad.

It makes little difference what we call it—false shame, or unhealthy
shame, or undeserved shame. It is all one feeling. The adjectives we
give it only reflect its different tones. Whatever we call it, we mean
to say that it is a shame we do not deserve to feel.

How can we know whether the shame we feel is healthy shame or
unhealthy shame? The feeling itself does not tell us. In a way, the
feeling is like a psychosomatic disorder; a blind person who has
nothing wrong with her eyes is as sightless as a person whose eyes

are neurologically dead. Likewise, a person who feels ashamed and has nothing to be ashamed of may actually feel the same way a person feels who has a lot to be ashamed of: my mother and Richard Malum.

Besides, most of us feel both healthy and unhealthy shame at different times, and sometimes both at once. Several layers of unhealthy shame may cover a deeper feeling of healthy shame. In fact, many of us need to heal our unhealthy shame precisely so that we can recognize and do something about the healthy shame underneath it.

All unhealthy shame is rooted in deceit of one sort or another. Bad people deceive themselves when they feel like virtuous people. Good people deceive themselves when they feel worse than they are. Either way, our feelings are out of synch with reality. However, it is hard to catch ourselves in the act of self-deceit. Nobody sets out to lie to himself; no one I know gets up in the morning and says to himself, "I think I shall tell myself a whopper of a lie today." The moment he lies to himself, he swears it is the truth.

In the past, I worried more about complacent people who were blind to their own shortcomings. Now I worry about shamed people who are blind to their own strengths.

The basic fact about undeserved shame is this: it is a false message from our false self.

Let me tell you what I mean by our false self. Our false self is an image of what we ought to be that is concocted out of false ideals. The false ideals are imposed on us by other people. They do not come from our true self, from the self we are meant to be. They are planted in us by sources that try to create us in their images. What sources? The most common sources of our false self are these three:

- secular culture
- graceless religion
- unaccepting parents

These three forces compete with one another to convince us that we need to measure up to their ideals if we are to be acceptable persons.

All three try to replace the ideal of our true self with their false image of the sorts of persons we should be. If we accept their image of the self we ought to be, we feel ashamed if we do not measure up to it.

Our secular culture tells us that if a person wants to be acceptable she must look good, feel good, and make good. The self we are supposed to be comes in a svelte body, draped in designer clothes, and capped with a gorgeous face. Further, she feels fantastic about herself; she feels seductive, alive, adorable, and wholly fulfilled. To top it off, she makes a lot of money and has considerable clout with important people. If we are too fat or too thin, too poor, and too powerless, our culture expects us to feel shame.

Graceless religion tells us that, to be acceptable, we must live up to the customs and shun the taboos of its tradition. It shames us when we do what it forbids and do not do what it requires. Our religion-shaped self easily becomes a self of hypocrisy and appearances; we feel compelled to make up for what we lack inside by obeying all its prescriptions on the outside. Graceless religion creates the illusion that if we only follow the letter of the rules, we will be acceptable, and that if we fail we will be rejected and despised.

Unaccepting parents impose a more complicated ideal on us. On the positive side, they tell us that, to be acceptable, we must win their approval by doing whatever they expect of us. On the negative side, they convince us that we are never going to be acceptable enough to meet their approval. They put us in a double bind: we know we must be very good if we are to earn their love, but we also know that we do not have it in us to be that good.

What makes it worse is that parents' requirements are usually unspecified. We must be fantastic abstractions. Unaccepting parents do not merely tell us that we must do our arithmetic, or treat the dog kindly, or wash our face clean; they tell us we must be an indefinably wonderful person. They do not merely criticize us for not doing our homework or messing up our rooms; they let us know that we are duds, just the opposite of what they want us to be, flops, maybe better off not born. Unaccepting parents signal to us that we are somehow indefinitely horrid and that to be acceptable we need to be just the opposite of the unspecified dolts we are.

We know in our hearts that nobody as bad as we are can ever be acceptable enough for unaccepting parents. As a result, we are stuck with shame we do not deserve.

Sometimes unaccepting parents are in cahoots with secular culture. Mark Ovachi, eleven years old, five feet four inches, is ashamed of himself. Why? He is short. How short? Shorter than his friends but about the same height as Milton Friedman, a Nobel Prize winner. An inch or so taller than Mickey Rooney. But he does not know who Milton Friedman and Mickey Rooney are. What he does know is that he is shorter than the other kids, and he is ashamed. So every night except Sunday his mother shoots a hormone into his arm to make his bones grow. The hormone costs her fifteen thousand dollars a year. But it is worth the price to her if it can heal Marco's shame. Meanwhile, Marco feels that if his mother goes to that much trouble, it must be because being short really is a shame, and so the cure gives birth to the disease.

In sum, the basic fact about unhealthy shame is that it is a false feeling inflicted by the false ideals implanted in us by secular culture, graceless religion, and unaccepting parents. If we let these false ideals become the image of the self we are supposed to be, we invite them to shame us. The shame we feel is false, and, what is worse, it often drowns out the messages sent from our true self.

It is terribly important to recognize the difference between our healthy shame and our false shame. However, the shame messages from our false self feel just like the shame messages from our true self. How can we know if our shame is an unhealthy shame we do not deserve to feel? Let me suggest a few symptoms.

Unhealthy Shame Exaggerates Our Faults

People who nourish unhealthy shame inside themselves are compulsive exaggerators. They have no sense for the distinction between minor misdemeanors and major felonies. A small blemish makes them feel like a giant gargoyle. A petty fault feels like moral cancer. Every trivial transgression feels to them like a capital case.

My wife, for instance, has a tendency to put off answering letters; I think it is because she feels as if every note she writes should be a model of profound thought come to life in lyrical elegance. Putting off writing letters may be a weakness, an annoyance sometimes, but not a wallop to the guts of anybody's moral ideal. Yet she sometimes feels as if a person who puts off writing a letter is as shameful as someone who steals poor people's social-security checks.

I tend to exaggerate my memories of insignificant failures as a father. For example, I remember getting cross at my boys on camping trips, losing my temper, especially after we had driven many miles looking for a site at which to pitch our tent. The bad memories make me feel like a perpetual crank who constantly spoiled family fun. My sons remember only the fun, but I remember the temper, and it makes me feel ashamed of myself even though I know that what I feel is unhealthy shame.

Unhealthy Shame Is Chronic

Most everyone walks through a valley of shame now and then. Some of us, however, take a lifelong lease on shame; it is our permanent home. We are shame-bound.

Our feelings are tilted toward shame. Anything can bring it on. A mild criticism of our work. A hunch that we are being overlooked when other people are set apart for honors. A memory of a foolish word we said to someone. Having a mistake pointed out to us. Anything the slightest bit negative sets us off. We are primed for shame—chronic cases.

Some of us are so hooked into shame that we are afraid we would be lonely without it. We have lived with it for so long that it has become part of our consciousness, part of ourselves, part of our being. If we lost our shame, we would not recognize ourselves. We feel toward our shame the way a person who has been in prison for forty years feels about his cell: he longs to be out of it and yet is frightened to leave it. The bad things we know often feel safer than the good things we do not know.

We are not prodigal sons who might come to our senses if we felt a shock of acute shame; we are the obedient sons who stay at home and still suffer the constant cramps of chronic shame.

Unhealthy Shame Is Put on Us by Others

False shame comes from outside; somebody taught us early on to accept false images of the self we are supposed to be. False shame comes to us from being violated or disowned or controlled by unaccepting parents. It comes from browbeating churches. It is put on us by a culture that shames us if we are not handsome, smart, and loaded with luxuries. It comes from what others tell us about what sorts of persons we ought to be, and for this reason alone it is a shame we do not deserve.

Unhealthy Shame Pervades Our Whole Being

Unhealthy shame spills over everything we are. We cannot get our shame on target. It flops, sloshes, and smears our whole being with the stain of unworthiness. It is a slovenly shame.

   Healthy shame is neat. It knows what it is after, and once it finds the shame spot, it zeroes in on it with a painful smack and lets the rest of our lives alone. But unhealthy shame has no aim, no focus; it leaves us feeling like *undefined, undifferentiated, free-floating failures*.

Unhealthy Shame Is Unspiritual

Spiritual shame may come as a tremor after a close encounter with God, but unhealthy shame is a godless shame. Undeserved shame may come from religion, but it only gets in God's way. Religion without grace can tie shame around our souls like a choke chain and never offer relief. The pain we feel is not even a distant cousin to spiritual shame.

Unhealthy Shame Makes Shame-bent People Proud of Their Shame

Shame-bent people often turn their shame into a twisted symptom of their own superiority. The reason they feel so much shame—they tell themselves—is that they judge themselves by divine standards.

Only very good people dare strive for virtue divine and by that token only very good people could feel so very badly about themselves for falling short of it.

The logic is convincing, if perverse. The shame-bent person reasons this way: Only someone with a profound nature and noble ideals could feel as rotten about himself as he does. So if you are happy, you must be a moral commoner, if not a moral clod, and you should be ashamed of yourself.

The Adams family of Quincy, Massachusetts, was proficient at this game. John Adams, second president of the United States, and his wife Abigail taught their children that they had a divine calling to walk the earth as moral examples for the masses who were disadvantaged by inferior moral training. The Adams children could not escape their burden; each one of them was haunted by a shaming voice he could not silence: You can never live up to your family's ideal. Some of them were driven by shame to alcoholism and suicide. A few, like John Quincy, were driven by shame to great distinction. But they all believed that they felt such shame only because they were people of unusual moral depth. If they, persons of such depths, were condemned to feel so much shame, the happy people of the world are shallow indeed and should be doubly ashamed of themselves.

I know a shame-driven man who tries to escape his shame by working hard enough to make himself acceptable to his hard-working father. But his inner demon is never satisfied; his shame is chronic. Since he cannot escape his shame, he uses it as proof that he suffers only because he is more conscientious than other people. His shame is a sign of his superiority and he wants his friends to know it.

He plays a mean game with them: he shames them by telling them how ashamed of himself he is. He whines: "I never seem to accomplish anything, never get anything done." Which means: "If I, who accomplish so much more than you do, if I am ashamed, the rest of you should feel worse than I do." But he has a friend who will not play his game. "I know what you are up to. You want the rest of us to feel rotten so that you can feel better about yourself. You use your humble shame to show how superior you are. Well, you are not going to fool me."

In this chapter I have described some of the characteristics of unhealthy shame. There are more, but these are enough to convince us that we do not deserve to suffer unhealthy shame and have every right to be rid of it. We shall come to the healing of our shame in good time. First, though, two other sides to shame invite us to look them over: spiritual shame and social shame.

Six

Spiritual Shame:
The Price We Pay to See God?

All the beauty of creatures compared to the infinite beauty of God is the height of ugliness. . . . All the grace and elegance of creatures compared to God's grace is utter coarseness and crudity. . . . And all the goodness of the creatures of the world compared to the infinite goodness of God can be called wickedness.

JOHN OF THE CROSS

I remember hearing Mahalia Jackson, the most serene of singers, comfort the weak creatures of the world with the good news that the Maker of heaven and earth kept his eye on every sparrow:

> I sing because I'm happy.
> I sing because I'm free.
> His eye is on the sparrow.
> And I know he watches me.

Mahalia comforted my fearful spirit: if God could care enough to keep his eye on the plainest of birds, he was surely watching over me. The feeling changed when a worried preacher warned me that God had his eyes on me. "You cannot hide behind a shade," he said, "because he is on both sides of every curtain. You cannot hide in the night because he is light itself. He sees everything. You have no hiding place." I was not comforted to know it.

Even my favorite psalm worries some people:

> O Lord, you have searched me and known me! You
> > know when I sit down and when I rise up;
> You discern my thoughts from afar.
> You search out my path and my lying down,
> And you are acquainted with all my ways.[1]

The prayers of the church, too, are a surrender to the all-seeing One: "O Lord, unto whom all hearts are open, all desires known, from whom no secret is ever hid." The jig is up. There is no point in denying anything.

It is not something I like to think of too often. Must everything be seen, filed away, pulled out to shame us when our time comes? The all-seeing Eye was certainly no comfort to Job: "Will you never take your eyes off me long enough for me to swallow my spittle? Suppose I have sinned, what have I done to you, you tireless watcher of mankind?"[2]

What can we do with this God who sees all and knows all? Nietzsche's idea was to get rid of him, so he invented a character who killed God. Someone asked the man why he killed God. The man said he had to. God knew too much: "He saw with eyes that saw everything; . . . all [my] concealed disgrace and ugliness. . . . He crawled into my dirtiest nooks. This most curious . . . one had to die."

But what if we cannot kill him off? And suppose, unkillable, he is a watchful Father who keeps his eyes on us, not to shame us but rather to save us and to be our friend. What then?

A snoop is one thing. A watchful parent is another. Is God like those hidden television cameras that stare day and night into every jail cell or scan every nook of the department store where we shop? Or is he more like a mother watching her toddler near a swimming pool and a father watching his daughter play the lead in *My Fair Lady?*

And what happens when the roles are switched? What if we are the ones who do the looking? What if we see him seeing us? Is shame our natural, proper feeling when we see God?

When saints and prophets had visions of God, they often came away with a feeling of shame. Take the prophet Isaiah, for example. What he saw when he saw the Lord was an unbearable Holiness. The opalescent wings of angels shaded the Unbearable Light while the seraphim flooded the temple with antiphonal sancti: "Holy, Holy, Holy is the Lord of Hosts." On seeing even his shaded Holiness, Isaiah felt like an unwashed beggar in the presence of a heavenly Queen:

> Woe is me! I am lost;
> for I am a man of unclean lips . . .
> my eyes have seen the King,
> the Lord of hosts.[3]

A person of unclean lips? Isaiah's lips spoke more sublimely, more elegantly, and more purely than any pair of lips in his world. How, then, could they be unclean? Isaiah was not suffering by a fair comparison with mortals like him; he had been stunned by incomparable Holiness. Even the purest person feels stained when she looks straight into Divine Purity.

Benedict Groeschel quotes a passage from the *Spiritual Letters of Archbishop Fenelon* to explain why people who see themselves in the Divine Light are so hard on themselves: "As light increases, we see ourselves to be worse than we thought. We . . . see issuing forth from the depths of our heart a whole swarm of shameful feelings. . . . We never could have believed that we had harbored such things." But Fenelon adds a hopeful touch: "We only see our malady when the cure begins."

Saints who get close to God often do get terribly down on themselves. People who have never gotten near God may suspect the saints of laying it on a bit thick, maybe doing some morbid grandstanding. Perhaps Augustine's rhetoric did run a step or two ahead of his real feelings when he wrote, "O Lord, thou didst set me face to face with myself that I might behold how foul I was and how crooked and sordid, bespotted and ulcerous. And I beheld and loathed myself."

Loathed himself? Is this a great teacher stretching the literal truth to dramatize his point? Maybe. But he may also be a discerning genius spotting rot within himself that coarser eyes miss, the way a musical genius hears sounds that coarser ears do not hear. When a genius sees himself in God's light, what he sees may well shame a saint.

I notice, too, that many hymns and much of the liturgy put the language of shame in the mouths of those who draw near to God.

The feeling of *unworthiness,* for example: "We are not worthy so much as to gather up the crumbs under thy table."

And a feeling of *emptiness:* "Truly there is no strength in us." "Nothing in my hand I bring; only to thy cross I cling."

Sometimes a feeling of *disgust:* "Would he devote that sacred head for such a *worm* as I?"

I wonder. Should we expect to feel this much shame whenever we get close to God? The way we expect to laugh when we go to see a comedy? We all have to discover for ourselves, I suppose, what it feels like to experience God. It may be that shame is just the right feeling to have—sometimes, anyway, depending on the shape we are in when God meets us, and depending, too, on which side of the divine mountain we approach.

I feel different when I get near to the divine side of God than I do when I meet the human side. When I grope for his Divinity, I feel shaken but not shamed. It is when I get in touch with his Humanity that I swallow a spoonful or two of healthy shame.

If I filter out all my feelings but those that matter here, I am left with these two:

- a feeling of smallness in contrast to the Divinity of God
- a feeling of shame in contrast to the Humanity of God

Now let me explain.

The Feeling I Get in the Presence of the Divinity of God

When I try to get close to God, he eludes me. He is always an Elusive Presence; he is here but never all here. I sense him around and under and over and in me, yet the moment I feel him, he slips away into an Immensity that I cannot locate or grasp. So near, so far—like any tomorrow, at my fingertips, but unreachable.

Now and then, awake, worrying in the dead of night, I plead with God to become more real, more available to me, so that I can siphon faith enough at least to trust my own children with him, and, while

I've got his ear, complain about the mess he has let his world get into, but he fades on me. Just when I feel he has gotten close, he becomes the wholly other again. But what should I expect, really? Every credible mystic has told us that the first thing one learns about divinity from the inside is that God keeps himself well hidden; count on it, if he isn't in hiding, he isn't God.

Sometimes I feel God's unshaped vastness with something like *awe*. Sometimes with fretting frustration. Now and then, not often, as a kind of *terror*—like the quirkish terror I feel when I stand at the foot of a tall building, and look straight up the sides of it. I think it would not feel all that different if I looked straight up the trunk of a Sequoia tree into the Divinity of God. I would feel as if I had lost my foundation, floating, with nothing to hold me up, and I would sink. Then the Elusive Presence would be there after all to hold me up, just when I felt the terror of his absence.

There is no shame in it. I do not feel shame when I feel small at the rim of the Grand Canyon or sluggish at the sight of a fleeting gazelle. I do not feel ashamed of the books I write because they are such meager things compared to the works of the great thinkers. Why should I feel shame when I feel my smallness next to God's infinity?

The Feeling I Get When I Experience the Humanity of God

Sometimes I feel the Humanity of God the way I feel when an old friend puts his arm around my shoulder, cordial, genial, even chummy, and tells me he is going to stick around and I should not worry. The Humanity of God stands for a God like us, and for us, God turning our way, getting close, becoming one of us. The human God could draw up a chair next to me anytime, talk my language, look at me eyeball to eyeball, on my level, not immense, not elusive, but touchable, knowable, lovable. The Humanity of God is what I meet in Jesus.

But there is a catch. When I get close to God, I do not feel small in contrast to Immensity or ugly in contrast to Divine Beauty. When I meet God in his Humanity, I am face to face with my own true self, and I feel a fierce dissatisfaction with the self I actually am for failing to be more of what I am meant to be.

I notice that Jesus never calculates the consequences before he speaks the truth; I feel a sudden pain about my self-protecting deceits. I see that he does what is right even when doing it will get him nailed to a cross; I feel a sharp pain at what a coward I am when it is risky to do the right thing. I sense how clearly he knows God's will and how he lets no sidetracks seduce him from it; I feel heavy about how easily I lose my way. I compare his love with mine; I am ashamed of my egoism and selfishness. The contrast between the Humanity of God and the humanity of Smedes shames me.

Spiritual shame, then, is the price I must pay for experiencing the friendship of the Human God. But recall the tag line to Fenelon's discovery of his own shadow side: "We only see our malady when the cure begins."

To make my point, I want to tell you about one of the best human beings I have ever known. His name was Lee Travis, the original dean of the school where I work. If you take the Bible's ideal of an excellent person—goodness joined to godliness—and then the Greek ideal of an excellent person—a healthy mind in a healthy body—and mix them thoroughly, you will get a Lee Travis. High-test humanity.

When I got close to Lee, I often felt acute dissatisfaction with myself. However, when I was in his presence for more than a few minutes, the shame left me. I felt better and more worthy for being with him. One ordinary day, when Lee and I crossed paths on campus as we had done on a hundred other ordinary days, he stopped me in my tracks with this revelation: "Lew," he said, "there are three men in my life whom I have deeply loved: one of them is Neil Warren, another is Louis Evans, and the other is you." The moment was a holy one for me, a holy, healing moment, when my shame was overcome by grace.

Lee's grace put me in touch with a beauty in myself that I would not have felt without it. So does the grace of the Human God. First I feel shame—that painful dissatisfaction with what I am when I get a clearer look at the self I am meant to be. But when God tells me he loves me, his grace heals the shame, and I feel more worthy than I did before.

This, in sum, is what spiritual shame feels like to me—a painful feeling of unacceptability in contrast to the self I see in the Humanity of God. However, the very pain is the onset of healing, for grace overcomes the contrast and makes me feel more worthy than if I had never felt the shame.

Let me recall the feelings again:

- a feeling of weakness, smallness, and dependence in contrast to his Divinity
- a feeling of shame in contrast to his Humanity

And now I will add a third—a new feeling of my own worth in the experience of his grace, the feeling of shame beginning to heal.

Seven

Social Shame: The Pain of Rejection

He was despised and rejected of men.

ISAIAH

Long before modern psychologists came along to discover it, ancient philosophers were curious about the shadow of shame that darkened the lives of so many people. What most interested them was the shame we felt when we were disgraced in the eyes of our own people. Take Aristotle, for instance; twenty-two centuries before the birth of Freud he observed that shame is what we feel when "we . . . are disgraceful . . . to those who care for us."

To be disgraceful to people who care for us means that our own people have no grace in their hearts for us. To be disgraceful is to be weighed and found unacceptable to those whom we need most to accept us. It is, in short, to be despised and rejected by our own. Is not this the shame we all fear most? Is it not the primal shame that we dread more than death itself? The label I am giving it here is social shame. There are three basic ways we can experience it.

- We experience shame if another person despises us as if we were nothing but objects to use instead of persons to love.
- We feel shame if we are despised and rejected by our own group.
- We feel shame when our group is despised and rejected by another group.

Let us explore each of these experiences.

We Are Shamed When Someone Looks on Us as If We Were Things and Not Persons

When another person looks us up and down the way a shopper inspects a chest of drawers, and then scorns us, he shames us because he makes us feel like nonpersons. It was this experience that so fascinated the existentialist philosopher Jean Paul Sartre who said that being looked on as an object is the essence of being shamed, the seed of the dehumanizing of humanity, and a feeling that triggers "an immediate shudder which runs from head to toe."

I knew a pretty good scholar once who was tormented every moment of his life by a "Cyrano complex." He knew in the depths of his heart that anyone who looked at him saw, not a person, but a huge, ugly nose. When I was a skinny boy sixteen years old and six feet three inches tall, I knew for sure that when anyone looked at me all she saw was a sharp pair of hip bones that stuck out of my sides like drawn swords.

It may be that nobody has captured this feeling as Dostoyevski did when one of his characters, Dmitri Karamazov, was on trial for his life. He was sitting in the dock, legs crossed, looking down at his dangling left foot as it wagged back and forth at the end of a ridiculously scrawny leg. His toe, grotesque knob that it was, a flat, gnarled, crooked, filthy object, poked its head out of a hole in his shoe! He knew for sure that everyone in the courtroom was staring at his toe, that they considered him to be worth no more than the worth of that obscene growth, and he loathed himself.

It can happen to anybody when someone else stares at her with contempt. A child feels it when his mother stares at him; her mouth says nothing, but her lips are taut with patience too much tested, and her eyes say, "I've had it with you, you miserable child." A man feels it when he goes to collect his first unemployment check and a person behind the desk glowers at him for one tenth of a second, looks at him with enough indifference to tell him he is a nobody, and then, eyes back at her papers, points her pencil at another line, and mutters, "Stand over there." A person who seldom eats at restaurants takes a table and feels disdain in the look of a man with a menu in his hand

and knows for sure that he is no more than a clod in the eyes of his waiter.

My friend Sandy is severely disabled, and people look at him as if all they saw in him was his physical difference. They wonder how he gets dressed, how he has sex, how he takes a shower, how he eats; sometimes they ask him. He feels shamed, and he spits the shame back at them: "It's none of your business."

Have you ever heard of the spitting cell? Albert Camus tells us about it in *The Fall.* The spitting cell is a walled closet high enough for a prisoner to stand up in but with no room for him to move his arms. There is a hole in the door at the level of his face. It is just big enough to show his face, but the shape of the closet prevents him from turning his head. Every time a jailer passes by he spits in the prisoner's face, and he sees to it that he walks by often. The prisoner cannot wipe his face; all he can do is close his eyes. Better for a proud man to die quickly.

One can see the mark of Cain in this light! There was no court to find him guilty for murdering his brother Abel. So God condemned him to shame. Cain had to wander the earth with something like a scarlet letter M scratched on his forehead. True, Cain's branding was to protect him as well as shame him; God promised to avenge sevenfold anyone who did him bodily harm. But by protecting him against killing, God made him suffer a shame worse than death. He was, in a way, condemned to spend his life in the spitting cell.

Job felt it too, rejected by God and despised by his people. God "has made me a byword of the peoples, and I am one before whom the people spat."[1]

Kase, secretary to the Japanese foreign minister, when he walked across the deck of the battleship Missouri to the table of surrender, stared at and despised by the crew felt like the man in the spitting cell. "Never have I realized that the glance of glaring eyes could hurt so much. We waited . . . in the public gaze like penitent boys . . . and every moment seemed ages."

The social experience of shame, then, is to feel that we are held up for inspection—by anyone at all—stared down, rejected, maybe spat at, as an object to scorn instead of a person to love.

We Are Shamed When Our Own People Reject Us

Shame digs deeper when it is our own people who reject us, who shame us because they feel shamed by us. Only people who are members of a community ever feel it, and only a community that cares for its members can effectively make them feel it. This is the paradox of all true communities: the closer knit and caring a community is, the more cruel its shaming can be.

When we were children, if one of us did something nasty, we would set him inside our circle, point our fingers at him, and sing this ditty:

> Shame, shame, double shame,
> Everybody knows your name.

We kept him in our circle but made him feel unworthy to be there.

"Everybody knows your name"; if nobody knew your name you would not feel the shame. It goes back to the primitive sense that a person's name stands for what people suppose she is. I remember my morbid fascination as I heard grown-ups gossiping about a man who had lost his good name. He still had a name, and everyone knew his name, but now it was a name with shame; he had become disgraceful in the eyes of those who cared for him, despised and rejected.

No one ever bore the pain of double shame more nobly than Hester Prynne—Nathaniel Hawthorne's tragic saint in *The Scarlet Letter*. Hester loved the good Reverend Arthur Dimmesdale, loved him well but not wisely, and became mother of his child. She was condemned for the rest of her days to wear a scarlet letter A on her bosom whenever she walked the paths of the village.

"Continually, and in a thousand other ways, did she feel the innumerable throbs of anguish that had been so cunningly contrived for her. . . . It could have caused her no deeper pang had the leaves of the trees whispered the dark story among themselves . . . had the wintry blast shrieked it aloud! . . . Hester Prynne had always this dreadful agony in feeling a human eye upon the token. . . ."

Despised and rejected by her own! If she had only been a stranger among strangers in Los Angeles, she could have worn her scarlet letter to church and hardly be noticed. One needs to belong to a real community to feel the shame of being shut out of it.

This is why a close-knit family that lives in a close-knit community is the most effective shamer of all. When a child is or does what the community considers shameful, the parents take the child's shame on themselves. In the process they inject their child with a double dosage of shame. In the old days, the parents hid the children; an unmarried daughter found with unwanted child was sent to the city to live with an aunt. Today, more often the child hides himself. A son discovers that he is homosexual and disappears from his family to avoid the pain of their shaming. People die of AIDS, alone, abandoned by their families. Shame is the dark side to what we extol as family values.

The beginning of the Gospel of John reveals the shame of Jesus in the same terms: "he came to his own home and his own people received him not." [2] In the end, they gawked at him in his dying as if he were a hog being slaughtered. But he refused to ingest into his own spirit the shame his people shamed him with. [3] In fact, Jesus turned the horror of social shame into an honor for those who are shamed for doing well. "Blessed are you when men hate you, and when they exclude you and revile you, and cast out your name as evil, on account of the Son of man!" [4]

Supremely good persons may be shamed in public and feel no shame within. But supremely wicked people also refuse to feel the shame of their shamers. They do it by deceiving themselves with the lie that they have nothing to be ashamed of. When Hitler's field marshall, Hermann Goering, sat in a row with the Nazi criminals and listened to lawyers recite the specifics of his evil life, he felt no shame. He leaned over to Albert Speer and said: "Never mind, in a few years they will build monuments in our honor." Goering was the type that Jeremiah, the saddest prophet, had in mind when he saw the shamelessness of the shameful: "They acted shamefully, they committed abomination; yet they were not ashamed; they did not know how to blush."[5]

One can be either too good or too evil to feel the shame of a community's shaming.

For those of us who are neither supremely good nor supremely evil, our sensitivity to social shame is a shield against our worse impulses. What keeps us on the straight and narrow is not so much fear of the judgment of God as the fear of being despised and rejected of men. Fear of shame is not the highest reason for suppressing our greed and controlling our passions, but it is an effective one. It may reflect the wisdom of Jefferson's unheroic prudence: "Act as if all the world were looking at you."

We Are Shamed When Our Group
Is Despised by Another Group

Shame, at one level, is the experience of feeling rejected by one's own group. On another level, it is the pain we feel when another group despises our group. We feel shame when our families are scorned by other families, our race by other races, our communities by other communities.

Our communities immunize us against shame with regular shots of community pride. When we celebrate our group's better ways, its nobler values, its more heroic history, and its glorious beginnings, we inject the pride of our community into our own bloodstream. As long as we keep our pride, like the Jew who taunted the Germans with a huge Star of David on his chest, we cannot be shamed by other groups. But the pride that protects us from shame also tempts us to shame people who belong to other groups.

The trouble begins when we persuade ourselves that our ways are the only right ways, that our religion is the only true religion, and that we are the best people of the world. It is the start of trouble because our pride in our group then tempts us to despise other groups, and to shame other persons simply because they are members of a group that our group despises.

Those we despise we are tempted to treat as despicable and disposable creatures. If my "superior" group believes that your "inferior" group is the cause of our group's troubles, we may exterminate you, as the Germans exterminated the Jews. If your "inferior" group stands in the way of our "superior" group's manifest destiny, we may destroy you, as European Americans destroyed Native Americans. If your ethnic group is weak and we need you, we may make slaves of you, as Americans did to Africans. If your group is hungry and your very existence challenges the selfishness of our rich group, we will turn our eyes from you and treat you as if you did not exist. If your ethnic group threatens to corrupt the purity of our ethnic group, we will, one way or the other, purify ourselves of your presence.

Slavery Is the Logic of Social Shame

Take slavery in America, for example. A slave was a slave for only one reason: he belonged to a group that was shamed by another group. A typical classified ad in a New Orleans newspaper of 1850 was a manifest of shame: "Negroes for sale - A negro woman 24 years of age, and two children, one eight and the other three years. Said Negroes will be sold separately or together as desired." Then, at the auction, the woman was lined up with other female slaves, separated from the males as heifers are separated from bulls, and put on the block.

A buyer would grab her chin and force her mouth open so that he could examine her teeth. He would feel her biceps and her thighs, and he might tell her to take her clothes off so he could see whether she had lashes on her back, a bad sign if she had them because they meant that she had to be whipped in order to keep her in line. And then she would be sold off, weeping for her children as she left them behind. But what did it matter? A slave's cries were no different from a pig's squeal or a wheel's squeak.

When I, in the pride of my group, despise another person simply because she is a member of a group that my group despises, I shame her. If I will not fellowship with you simply because you belong to a group that my group considers inferior, I shame you. When I will not allow you to have the same rights that I have simply because you belong to a group that I think threatens the privileges of my group, I shame you. I have reduced you; I have turned you into a nonperson with no identity but the name of the group that my group despises. I have taken the first step that, in other days, could have made of you a slave.

Social shame is the pain that comes to people who live together and yet despise one another. We feel it when one other person treats us with contempt as if we were nothings. We feel it when our community rejects and despises us. We feel it when another community rejects and despises our community. It may be that all the shame we feel inwardly, alone, in the privacy of our souls, is rooted in the fear of being shamed by other people. For this reason, the simplest of all remedies for shame is the discovery that we are in spite of everything accepted by the grace of someone we most need to accept us.

Eight

Our Sense of Shame:
Keeper of Our Mysteries

The function of shame is to preserve wholeness and integrity.

CARL SCHNEIDER

I am waiting to be loaded on an airplane, and I watch the ceaseless march of hurried and tired travelers, their dilapidated or sometimes sculpted bodies slouching and striding to their boarding gates. I imagine that they are all naked, and I silently thank a considerate Creator for telling Adam and Eve to put on some clothes. It is no offense to our body's Maker to say that most of us look better when our bodies are draped.

But important as clothes are to what we look like, they are more deeply the metaphors of what we are. They are signs of our mystery, and mystery is the sign of a real self:

> If we have no privacy, we have no mystery, and if we have no mystery we have no self.

> If we have no privacy, we have no depth: we are on the surface, transparent, superficial, shallow, boring.

> If we have no privacy, we have no sacredness: we lose our boundaries, and we have no place within that is holy to ourselves. Take away our sacredness, and we lose our core.

If we have no privacy, we lose our identity: it is swallowed in the mass. We do not know who we are even if we are celebrities and everybody on earth knows our name.

Our human need for privacy is different from our desire for secrecy. We keep secrets to conceal facts; we need privacy to conceal ourselves. People love secrecy, the Bible says, because their deeds are evil, but people love privacy if their deeds are honorable. We protect our secrets from those who want to see what we have done. We protect our privacy from those who want to see what we are.

People differ in their feelings about privacy because they differ in their feelings about themselves and about what is vital to their mysteries. Some anthropologists believe there is a universal consensus about what is private: most cultures keep private the body functions that come closest to the essence of our biological existence: being born, making love, and dying.

But eating, too, is a private thing for many people. Anthropologists tell us about tribes in which people walk naked through the village but families never eat in public. With us it depends on the occasion; we gobble a hot dog in a crowd at the ball park, but we do not want a stranger looking over our shoulders while we eat dinner at home with our family.

Most of us still feel that making love is a private affair. It needs to be private because it is a moment for revelation. If we do not reveal ourselves, we do not make love; we only have sex. Only private people *can* make love because only people with mysteries have anything to reveal.

The bathroom is usually the only room in the house with a lock on the door. The lock is a metaphor of a human need for privacy. Not only to discharge and cleanse our bodies unseen, but to relieve our spirits, too. I remember how, on Saturday night, when she was hanging on to the frayed edges of her staying power after another tough and lonely week, her five kids squabbling in the kitchen, my mother went to the bathroom to weep. We need one room with a lock on the door where we go to be one with our mystery.

The story of life's beginning speaks to us of the link between privacy and shame. Adam and Eve walked naked with God in the cool of the garden and felt no shame. They were not shameless; they had a keen sense of shame. It was just that nakedness did not make them feel shame. They felt no shame because they felt perfect trust. When they lost trust they felt shame. And so it was that "the Lord God made for Adam and his wife garments of skin, and clothed them."

When they learned to trust each other, they could be naked to each other again, unashamed, but then alone, trustingly, in the soft shadows away from strangers who were not partners in their trust.

This is the tension that creatures with a sense of shame live in always. Our need for privacy is always balanced by a need to be naked—of body or of soul—in the risky security of perfect trust. Our sense of shame keeps the balance intact. We are ashamed to be exposed in public. We long to expose ourselves in trusting love.

Pornographers are shameless. This does not mean that—like Adam and Eve—they are unashamed; it means that they have lost their power to feel shame. To that extent, they have lost their souls. You lose your feel for mystery when you lose your soul.

Being punished in public can be worse than being naked in public. The parents of a slave family being lashed before their children suffered a shame more painful than the whip, and how terrible it is for a boy to be spanked in front of his friends.

When I was a boy, and I was hanging around, sluggish, dreaming about nothing in particular, my tongue had a tendency to droop out of the side of my mouth. The sight of my languid tongue annoyed my mother considerably, drove her, in fact, into a moment of madness. One early August evening, close to my seventh birthday, I was sprawled out on a porch swing, taking in some grown-up gossip going on between my mother and some neighbors who had stopped out front to pass the time. I yielded my torpid mind to the toneless murmur. My jaw sagged, and my tongue slid outside of my mouth without any thought of going anywhere, just dangling there like the soft end of a limp belt. My mother caught the tongue in the corner of her eye, and it was too much for her. She raised her arm, unleashed the back of her hand, and caught me where my tongue and I hung in front of the world.

I did not move an inch. Didn't bawl. Didn't complain. I felt only a deep deserving; I must have had it coming. Anyone with a hopeless tongue like mine must deserve to be smacked in public. I swallowed my mother's shame of me and digested it inside of myself until it was all mine.

Dying is even more private than punishment. As we approach the ultimate experience of our mortality, the sting of death, we have a primitive need to preserve the mystery of that moment by dying in private. We do not like to die all alone. Nobody wants absolute privacy, ever, but we also do not want to die behind the display window of a department store. We want people around us when we die whom we trusted with our mysteries while we lived; we want family, trusted friends, children, parents, but nobody else around us when we enter the dark passage. Again, it is trust that draws the circle inside of which we are willing to share our most private selves with others.

Some people think that we should televise executions for the same reason they used to hang pickpockets in the public square. In this way, we could make the criminal feel the shame as well as the judgment. Even now, murderers on death's row sometimes fear being gawked at while they die as much as they fear death itself. Maureen McDermott, for instance, who, as I write, is waiting to die at San Quentin prison, said that what she dreads is not dying itself so much as dying in front of a dozen gaping witnesses. If we killed Maureen McDermotts on television, we would compound the shame by a factor of thousands.

There is also a shame in the nakedness of the eye, which explains the ancient taboo against a stranger looking straight into the eyes of another. A person who stares like a voyeur without love into someone's eyes shames her soul.

My friend Naomi has been totally blind for about fifteen years. One morning I chatted with her when she had just come back from a vacation in Australia. She was enchanted by the visit and relished telling me about it. I, in turn, was fascinated that someone could feel so much delight in visiting a land that lay in total darkness to her. While we were talking, a woman came and told Naomi that she was praying that God would do a miracle and heal her eyes. Naomi said that the woman needn't bother.

I asked her, "Why not? Why don't you want her to pray for you to see?"

"There are some things I would miss if I got my sight back."

"Things you would miss if you could see?"

"Yes, for one thing, I think I'm becoming a better person than I was when I could see."

"Is that it?"

"No, there's more."

"What else would you miss?"

"Privacy."

"Being blind gives you privacy?"

"People don't look in my eyes."

"You don't want to feel people looking in your eyes?"

"No, I don't. When I could see, I knew when people were looking into my eyes, and I felt that they could see straight through me. Now I can talk with people and I am not afraid of their eyes anymore."

The eyes are the windows of the self. I am oddly reminded of a young woman named Claudia who gave her life to the ballet. She was starving while she waited for her chance to dance so she took a job in the chorus line of an off-Broadway musical. The show had one scene in which the dancers in the line dropped their costumes to the floor. She dropped hers on cue, felt the stares of strangers on her body, was seized by shame, and she covered . . . her eyes.

A person can be shamed not only by being seen but also by seeing what is shameful to see. There are fierce and unforgiving taboos rooted in ancient intuitions against a son seeing his parent's naked-ness. Ham, recall, was cursed for looking on the nakedness of his fa-ther, Noah.

I saw my mother's nakedness once, and it shamed me. Her nurses and I were having a hard time of it lifting her inert body back onto her hospital bed. Broken hip. Dead weight. Heavy woman anyway. Earlier in the afternoon, when she had enough spunk to help us, we had slid her from her bed into a wheelchair. However, as the afternoon hours wore on, and we had talked too long of things that used to be, her pepper was all spent, and her body sank into itself.

Two nurses and I manipulated my mother's limp bulk out of the chair and pushed it out of reach. We lost our grip on her, and she began to crumple. An orderly passed by, and we yelled for him to come in. He stooped down behind her, got his back beneath her bottom, and, like one of those hydraulic hoists, pushed her up to the edge of the mattress while the nurses and I tried to get her body stretched across the length of the bed to its place of comfort and rest. The nurses pulled her by the armpits while I, at the foot of the bed, put my arms around her thighs and shoved her upward toward the pillow. By that time her gown was twisted around her midsection, leaving the lower half of her naked.

The shame I felt felt right to feel.

In sum, our sense of shame may be one of the most critical defenses of our personal mystery and personal depth. This is all the more reason, then, to keep to ourselves a private preserve where no one else— except people bonded to us in committed trust—may come in. We show a healthy respect for our own selves when we keep our material and spiritual clothes on most of the time. When Jesus told his followers to get themselves inside a closet when they bared their souls to God, he revealed an uncommon sensitivity to the need for privacy that keeps alive our link to divinity.

PART THREE

The Sources of Shame

Nine

How Our Parents Can Shame Us

*If Garp could have been granted one vast and naive wish, it would
have been that he could make the world safe for . . . children.*

JOHN IRVING

A man I know disowned his children. When I learned what he had
done, I thought that he had decided not to leave his children any of
his money, of which he had more than his share, after he died. But this
is not what he really meant. He meant to purge them from his life,
make it official that he despised and rejected them.

Disowning a child is the sure way to get a child to feel that he is not
worth owning. The tragedy of being disowned is compounded by
the fact that very decent people disown their own children. They
may not do it totally, and they may not tell anyone about it. They
may do it in bits and pieces, with facial expressions, chiding voices, and
pious rebukes, without ever saying, "I disown you." However, they get
the message across to their children as clearly as if they announced it
in the newspaper.

If I am going to make clear what I mean by disowning a child, I need
to tell you what I mean by owning our children. I wish I had a better word for it. I am afraid that when I talk about "owning," I may
sound as if I am talking about "possessing" a child. But owning is not
the same as possessing.

If we possess something, we can control it, use it, neglect it, and get
rid of it as the mood strikes. This is why only lifeless things may be

possessed. But if we own a person, we give her our commitment of an unconditional love and thereby tell her that she will never be disowned, never rejected, never despised.

The difference between owning and possessing comes down to this: we possess things, but we own persons. We do whatever we wish with what we possess. We treat a person we own as the Godlike and therefore inviolable being he or she is. Possession is control; ownership is commitment.

It seems to me that to own a child means at least these three things:

- Taking responsibility: I respond to my child's deep need to be owned with a commitment that we will always belong to each other.
- Feeling pride: I am eager to let the world know that this child and I belong to each other.
- Finding joy: I am grateful and elated that this wondrous human being is here with me and I am here with her.

Two of my friends gave me a tender hint recently of what it means to own a child.

Esther and Max De Pree's granddaughter was a wee thing when she was born; she weighed one pound and seven ounces, and, as Max describes her, she was "so small that my wedding ring could slide up her arm to her shoulder." The child's natural father had deserted his family a little while before she was born. The medical team gave her a 5 to 10 percent chance of living three days.

The nurse in the intensive-care unit gave Max some firm instructions. He shares them in his splendid book *Leadership Jazz*. I share them here as the key to ownership:

> For the next several months, at least, you're the surrogate father. I want you to come to the hospital every day, . . . and when you come I would like you to rub her body and her legs and arms with the tip of your finger. While you're caressing her, you must tell her over and over how much you love her, because, you see, she has to be able to connect your voice to your touch.

The baby survived, thank God, and bears the name Zoe—a Greek word that means *life*. I do not know what it means for newborn children to feel feelings, but I am absolutely sure they feel them.

What did Zoe feel? The touch and voice of loving ownership. These, I am sure, made her feel belonged to, accepted, and owned by the loving people who made their commitment to her with touch and voice.

Feeling owned—I am free to make four fundamental discoveries about myself:

- I am someone who has been loved from the beginning by the person who gave me life.
- I am someone to whom someone else made an unconditional commitment from the beginning.
- I am someone whose parents consider me worthy of the love they give.
- I have the power to own myself: I take responsibility for my life, I am proud to be who I am, and I have joy in being myself.

Feeling owned, I contend, is love's way to immunize a child against shame. Now I want to explain how feeling dis-owned is the seed-bed of shame.

The most obvious way for a parent to disown a child is to be unable to take responsibility for her.

Cathy, my daughter, felt disowned by the mother who conceived her, carried her, gave her birth, and then gave her to Doris and me for adoption. Cathy knew in her mind that having been given for adoption as a baby had nothing to do with her worth as a woman, but what she felt, not what she thought, is what made it a special challenge for her to own herself. Her feelings told her: if I had been worth it to her, my mother could have found a way to keep me: "Would she own me now if she could see me? I need to find out."

Cathy was determined to find her birth mother but was discouraged at the start. The people at the adoption agency told her that her mother by birth had never called, never written, never asked what had happened to her baby. Cathy told me about how she felt.

"Dad," Cathy said, "she never even asked about me. Didn't care enough to pick up a phone and make a call, didn't care where I went and what happened to me."

Who knows how many people of infinite worth cannot own themselves with pride and joy because somebody did not have the resources to take responsibility for them?

A parent can disown a child in bits and pieces, too.

Someone has marketed a kind of pillow-sized mitt with a thick thumb in it where a baby's bottle can fit. A mother can snuggle her child up to the bottle and get him fed without the touch and voice of loving ownership. The people who make that mitt will make it a little easier for harried mothers to disown their children, if only for a while.

The children will pay with shame.

A parent's inability to take pride in ownership is a more subtle but no less real way to disown a child.

A tired and discouraged parent can be unable to take pride in a child—if only for one critical moment—because she does not have power to take pride in herself.

One Sunday, when I was a boy, a few brothers and sisters in the faith dropped in at our house for a visit after the evening service at our church. I sat alone in our darkened kitchen, ears cupped at the keyhole of the door that separated the kitchen from the living room, catching what I could of their benign gossip about the sick and erring members of the congregation.

By and by, they shifted to some modest bragging about their children. Better-than-average children they all were, growing up nicely, well on their way to making something of themselves in the world of real Americans.

My mother must have wished to God she had it in her to be a booster for her own brood the way her friends boostered theirs. However, her gentle demons drove her to run us down: we were not too bright, did not do what we were told, wore out our clothes too fast, and caused her a lot of worry. I heard what she said, and I slunk to bed like a disowned child.

This magnificent woman prized us more than she valued her own life. When her husband collapsed one Monday morning and died at the age of thirty-one, she was caught without any job skills, without a brother, sister, or cousin on the continent, not able to write

English and hardly able to speak it, and without any social welfare. What she did have were five rambunctious little ones whose mouths she filled three times a day by scrubbing strangers' floors. She was only thirty, but she put every honorable desire and every need native to a woman's heart on hold so that she could give us what we needed.

My mother took responsibility for us heroically, but why could she not own us with pride in front of her neighbors? I know the answer, and it is a sad thing to know: she did not dare take pride in us because she did not dare take pride in herself. Why did this great woman feel so depleted of self-worth?

My mother's circumstances were enough to crush a person's pride. She was all alone, terribly tired, and very poor—enough to depress anybody. Then there were her religious neighbors, who believed that it was their calling to persuade her that she was not up to rearing five children who were already showing signs of being nothing to be proud of. But millions of people have kept their pride under even worse circumstances. What handicapped her went deeper.

I learned about it years later, while my mother was still alive, from her older sister Jeltje; she was the first kin of my mother I had ever met, and she was a living copy. When I was in the Netherlands for graduate studies, I went up to see her at her farm in Friesland as soon as I had learned some Dutch in Amsterdam. Frisian is not the same thing, but we got along wonderfully, she with the Dutch she remembered from school and I with the Frisian I remembered from my mother. She gradually trusted me with her memories, and one memory unlocked others the way a sluice gate once opened unlocks the water of a Frisian canal. She remembered some beautiful and some horrible things.

I will tell you only this: my mother had a demented stepfather who apparently, when she first showed signs of ripening, went crazy at the sight of her. He repeatedly, day after day, grabbed her by her hair, lifted her off her feet, and beat her with his fists. The sin of the father becomes the shame of the daughter, and the shame of the daughter shrivels her power to take pride in herself.

Once I knew the secret, I never again wondered why my mother did not have enough faith in herself to take pride in her children. I wonder instead how a child so shamed at the start could shine so fine in the end. As I wonder, I think I hear the answer blowing in the winds of grace.

Finally, consider how parents can disown a child simply by showing no joy in her existence.

Sheila and Lambert Schaam had one secret shame of their own that flowed into all of their child's feelings about herself.

They lived in favor with God and man at the Church of Fundamental Truth. But Sheila Schaam felt a secret shame for an unholy stream of sexual desire that flowed too strong for comfort in the shadows of her saved soul. When she was beyond the time women in her circles properly conceived, Sheila became pregnant, and it was not long before everyone in the congregation could see that she and Lambert had—at their disgusting age—been up to something.

Elizabeth was born as the child of their shame. From the start, Sheila and Lambert made it clear to Elizabeth that they took no joy in her existence. She knew early on that she was an unwanted child whom her parents did not want to own. Since she knew she was only an unclean piece of freight they had to lug into old age, she determined to live the sort of life that matched a child whose very existence was a shame to her parents.

At seventeen Elizabeth rode off into her wilderness on the lambskin seat of a Harley Davidson with a 280-pound cyclist who had mastered the skills of making a woman feel unworthy. She lived with him for a brutal year or so, long enough to add a smashed nose, two abortions, and an off-again, on-again drug habit to her undeserved shame. All the while, her shame convinced her that she deserved no better.

We can, I believe, state it as a law of life: disown a child, and when she is older she will disown herself.

A more common way to disown a child is to make sure that whenever she gets caught being a nuisance, she understands that she is a joyless pain in the neck, the breaker of a mother's heart, by saying things like this:

How could you cause me so much pain, your mother, who sacrifices *everything* for you?

Who do you think you are? You're nothing but a sniveling brat. Why can't you ever do anything to please your parents?

Can't you ever, ever get anything into your thick head? You are so stupid, you make me sick.

Even if the lyrics only say, "Cut it out; you are giving me a headache," the music says, "You are unacceptable; I wish you were not my child."

Fathers who look and act like the Lord hurling the law from Mt. Sinai are expert at making a child feel like an unworthy object it is no joy to own. Strong male gods, the kind who take no joy in masculine weakness, have a natural talent for shaming a sensitive boy. General Douglas MacArthur, supreme commander of the United States Army, became a god to the Japanese people and a distant deity to his son, Arthur. But the general loved hard things like guns and medals and, though he loved his son, he felt shame for the soft music and poetry that Arthur loved.

When his god died, Arthur disowned his father's famous name, bore his shame into his own secret wilderness, and followed his music unnoticed and unknown in the great godless city.

All parents feel like disowning their children once in a while. Children can be such nuisances. They are ruthless; they act as if they possess us and can treat us like slaves, as if we had nothing else in the world to do but make them comfortable. They are jealous of us; the moment we pay attention to another person, they scream to get our focus back on them. They spit out the good food we give them, and they will not be quieted when they feel like crying.

We do not always have the emotional energy for taking responsibility for such nuisances, and our children do not always make us proud or give us joy to have them about. We yell at them. We tell them to go away. We all have made mistakes with our children that we look back on with shame and wish to God we had not made.

But sometimes there is a pattern. A prevailing mood. Some parents hardly ever assume responsibility, hardly ever display any pride, or hardly ever feel any joy in a child. When their failure is consistent, when they seldom give the voice and touch of love, their child gets a certain signal that, in at least some ways, she or he is disowned. When a child feels disowned from one day to the next, she blames herself. If she is not owned by her parents, it can only be that she is not nice enough, good enough, beautiful enough to be worth owning. Not by them and, consequently, not by herself.

This is what unhealthy shame is about, feeling we are not worthy of being owned. Or of owning ourselves. This is why, when we are healed of shame, the surest sign of health is the power to own ourselves again.

Ten

How the Church Fed My Shame

*The Church proclaims the grace of God. And moralism, which is the
negation of it, always creeps [back] into its bosom. . . . Grace
becomes conditional. Judgment appears. . . . I see every
day its ravages in . . . all the Christian Churches.*

PAUL TOURNIER

A person can catch a healthy case of shame at church. She can also find
healing for her shame there. This is the way it should be. The church
is meant to be a place where we get the courage to feel some healthy
shame and the grace to be healed of it.

But sometimes people come to church carrying a load of unhealthy
shame and their burden gets heavier for having come. Their unhealthy shame blocks their spiritual arteries and keeps grace from
getting through. And when it finally comes, the word of grace they
do hear sounds more like judgment than amazing grace. The sweet
hour of prayer becomes an hour of shame.

How does it happen? I can only tell you how it happened to me.
Maybe my story will remind you of yours, but then again your experience may have been very different from mine. I am not going to
draw any conclusions about other churches. I want only to recall
what I *felt* at mine.

I remember hearing three voices in the church. Each of them, as
I heard it, and each in its own way, fed the shame I brought with me
to church.

The voice of duty: God required me to be perfect before
I could be acceptable to him.

The voice of failure: I was flawed, worse than imperfect,
and all in all a totally unacceptable human being.

The voice of grace: by the grace of God I could be forgiven for my failure.

First, then, a word about how I heard the voice of duty. I felt that
I had a duty to be perfect the way God is perfect. Jesus himself said
so: "You must, therefore, be perfect as your Father in heaven is perfect." The general impression this left me with was that I had to be
like Jesus, not now and then, but all the time.

> Be like Jesus, this my song,
> In the home and in the throng,
> Be like Jesus all day long,
> I would be like Jesus.

I was not sure whether I wanted to be like Jesus all day long. Nor
did I have a clear notion of what it would take for a puny kid like me
to be like an ancient Jewish rabbi on his way to being the Savior of
the world.

I did understand that the only way for me to become like Jesus all
day long was to be truly born again. So I was born again; it happened
when I was about twelve or thirteen years old. I do not recall that
the experience gave me much joy. In fact, being born again added to
my shame. I figured that my folks would expect a born-again boy to
be like Jesus all day long, in the home and in the throng—and I could
not see myself becoming that good so soon.

It happened this way. I tagged along on Sunday afternoons with
my older brother, Wes, and some of his friends to a mission Sunday
school on the other side of town where they evangelized boys and
girls with considerable zeal. After we sang some fine gospel songs and
listened to a Bible lesson, they clustered us into small circles, where we
put our heads down and prayed for Jesus to come into our hearts.

One summer Sunday, sitting in my circle, I became so sad about the
prevailing shamefulness of my life that I broke down and cried. The
teacher put a caring arm around my shoulders:

"What is on your heart, Lewis?"

I knew what he was hoping for, and I said what I thought he would want me to say: "I've never been born again before, and I just got born again."

"Praise the Lord. Oh, yes, praise the Lord, Lewis. The angels are rejoicing in heaven right now for you, Lewis."

Maybe the angels were celebrating, but I began to feel edgy about it the moment I spoke the words. I guessed that my teacher would share the good news with my brother and that he would spill the beans to the rest of my family. I knew that they would keep a weather eye on me and let me know as soon I showed signs of being somewhat less than a born-again boy was expected to be.

One night a couple of weeks later, feeling more miserable than usual about the way life was shaping up for me, I decided to run away from home. I ran as far as the crawlspace under the back stoop of our house, where I crouched for an hour or so, time enough for me to figure out that misery in my own bed might have an edge over misery under the stoop.

I strolled back into the house, nonchalantly, as if I had just been out for a look at the stars. But I knew what was coming, and it came right away, from my older sister. She offered it casually without lifting her head from a book she was reading, as if my fall was what anyone would have expected.

"Soooo, you are the kid who claims to be born again!"

My sister echoed the second message that I heard at church: the fact that I should feel ashamed for my failure to be the sort of person that a born-again boy was duty bound to be.

I felt a lot of shame for running away from home only two weeks after I was born again, but the shame I felt about the fantasies that trickled through my born-again head while I was tucked away in my own bed was far worse. Of course, it is possible that I was not really born again at all. Maybe I just did not want to disappoint my Sunday school teacher. Then again, maybe I did make a sputtering start at being a born-again boy. In any case, my shame was now compounded because, in addition to my normal failures, I was now a hypocrite.

The shame I felt was not—for the most part—a very spiritual experience. The feeling did not come from a firsthand experience with

God so much as from a firsthand experience of my boyish humanity. When I heard at church that I was a sinner through and through, I only felt my old shame for all the natural goings on inside my body. I supposed that my biological shenanigans registered in heaven with the same clank as robbery and mayhem.

The third message was the good news that Jesus died for my sins, and I could be saved by grace. Hearing this message was the most perplexing part of my church experience. Grace, I knew, was good news, but the good news did not feel good to me. The good tidings of great joy made me sad. Grace felt heavy to me.

The good news of grace came only after the bad news that I was mired in sin's clotted clay. I know now what the strategy was: the bad news was meant to get me to feel so hopelessly flawed that I would be that much more grateful for the grace of God when it got to me. But, in fact, my spiritual malaise linked up with my chronic feeling of shame for being human, and the two of them brought forth in me a mess of homogenized shame, healthy and unhealthy, all mixed together. By the time the good word got to me, I was sunk so deep in my shame that I could feel no lightness in grace.

Another thing that made grace seem heavy was the church's preoccupation with guilt. Grace flowed from Jesus as pardon for the sins I was guilty of committing. But guilt was not my problem as I felt it. What I felt most was a glob of unworthiness that I could not tie down to any concrete sins I was guilty of. What I needed more than pardon was a sense that God accepted me, owned me, held me, affirmed me, and would never let go of me even if he was not too much impressed with what he had on his hands.

Still another thing that made grace feel heavy to me was my bounden duty to be grateful for it. Grace was so rich and God was so good that it was my bounden duty to be overflowing with gratitude for them both. Indeed, my main goal in life was to show how grateful I was.

The summons sounded very reasonable to me. My problem lay in my feelings: I found it hard to feel grateful for a gift when I was constantly reminded of how unworthy I was to get it. Anybody will feel shame at being an unworthy beggar even if he gets rewarded for admitting he is one, and I felt like the least worthy beggar of all.

The burden of gratitude got heavier as I felt the enormity of the debt. The songs we sang made the burden no lighter:

> I gave, I gave my life for thee.
> What hast thou given to me?

Never enough, oh, Lord, never enough. How can an imp of a boy with a soiled soul ever give enough to repay so great a debt?

I used to dream that one day when I really did become a born-again Christian I would become a missionary and go to Africa, where they would boil me in a pot and eat me for dinner. At last, if I could only arrange to be eaten for Christ, I would be worthy. Short of that, I supposed, I would always be shameful for my lack of gratitude.

We sang a ditty in Sunday school that went like this:

> I've got the joy, joy, joy, joy
> down in my heart,
> down in my heart to stay.

But I did not have it—not to stay, hardly for a moment. What I did have was a chronic case of shame.

Was the shame I felt at church a healthy shame? A shame I deserved? Or was it an unhealthy shame—the kind I didn't deserve? "Was my sinful self my only shame"? No, I was ashamed of my good self, too.

My healthy shame and my unhealthy shame were melted down into a glut of unworthiness, and the good word of grace never swam its way into my heart through the spiritual sludge.

I have since learned that the amazing grace that saved a wretch like me brings with it the discovery that I am worthy of the grace that saves. I know that wretches like me do not *deserve* amazing grace; it would hardly be amazing grace if we had it coming. But we can be worthy of it even though we do not deserve it. This is what grace can reveal.

This, as I recall it through the gauze of selective memory, was how I fed my shame at church when I was growing up, one young man, already muddled with shame. I hope that my story has stirred your memory of your own story, and I hope that your story is happier than mine.

Eleven

How We Shame Ourselves

The self-deceiver . . . both believes and does not believe
[what he says] . . . or he would not be self-deceived.

PHILIP LEON

The capacity for healthy shame is a gift. The experience of unhealthy shame is a curse. We do not deserve it; but we *are* coresponsible for nurturing it into a chronic pain.

No doubt many of us suffer shame we do not deserve because of what other people have done to us. Our parents may have shamed us, and our religious groups may have nurtured what our parents planted. We may also be programmed for shame by our genetic codes. But we are, I believe, responsible for what we do with what other people did to us.

When it comes right down to it, cruel as it sounds, we suffer the shame we do not deserve because we deceive ourselves. We deceive ourselves with the falsehood that we are unworthy human beings. We support our deception with plausible reasons why we *should* feel unworthy. We pollute our consciousness the way a factory manager may release toxic chemicals into a stream and immediately convince himself that the stream is where he *should* release them. This is why we usually need outside help, divine and/or human, to uncover our own self-deceit.

We lie to ourselves to hurt ourselves. Our deceit steals our joy and makes us spiritually heavy. Why, then, do we do it? If we knew the answer with precision, we would decipher the mystery of much needless misery. However, if we can recognize a pattern in our deception, we may understand at least some of the reasons why we hurt ourselves so much, and if we can also see beyond what we do into why we do it, we will be that much closer to healing.

Let me suggest some of the artful dodges that shame-prone people use to trick themselves into unhealthy shame. If you are shame-prone, I am sure you will be able to add some tricks of your own.

Shame-Prone People Discount Their Positives

People who suffer undeserved shame could hear a choir of five hundred voices sing an anthem to their good qualities and deny that they heard a word of it. They hear honest compliments and discount them before they sink in. They tell themselves that people who praise them are not sincere, or that if those people really knew the truth they would not say the nice things they say about them, or that the virtues they praise are really of no account. They always find a way to disqualify whatever good other people see in them.

If they are highly successful people and the evidence of their success is undeniable—no matter what it is they are successful at—they inwardly discount their own success. They discount it because every mountain climbed leaves them with five still to climb. More success will not heal their shame any more than drinking more cola will nourish a starving person.

If we ask why shame-prone people's bright success is seldom enough to lift their burden of shame, we get a simple answer: their search for success is spiritually misdirected. They do not seek success as a means of doing the world some good. They seek it as a proof that they are worthy persons—worthy, that is, by the false standards of worthiness that their false self imposes on them. But no success can satisfy the insatiable appetite of their false self; their pursuit is endless, and shame is their life's burden.

Shame-Prone People Magnify Their Flaws

Shame-burdened people inflate their negatives just as they discount their positives. Anything less than stunning success is miserable failure. They do not believe in minor faults; any surface flaw makes them fundamentally unacceptable.

Religious people seem especially vulnerable. They assume that since their human goodness amounts to little compared to God's goodness, their human goodness is only badness with a respectable sheen.

Why do shame-burdened people persist in magnifying their flaws? For many reasons, one supposes, but mainly because early on they learned that the only significant thing about them is their flawed nature. They were permitted to know only their flaws, their fatal flaws. Nothing good or true or beautiful about them was worth noticing. No smudge was too small to ignore. The least of their weaknesses outweighed the greatest of their strengths. The lesson was: every unwanted fleck was enough to condemn them. The reward for learning their lesson was a lifelong burden of shame.

Shame-Prone People Judge Themselves by Undefined Ideals

Shame-prone people are dogged by unrelenting but unspecified obligations to be perfect in some shapeless way, and, since no one can ever live up to ideals that no one can describe, they doom themselves to be haunted by failure.

Why do shame-prone people burden themselves with impossible ideals? One reason may be their fear of pride. If they accept specific ideals for themselves, they might succeed and feel pride in their achievement. However, pride is precisely what they cannot allow themselves; the voice of their shame tells them that they are not worthy to feel any pride in themselves. So they take on ideals they cannot define to guarantee that they will never achieve them. In this way they see to it that shame will be the major theme in the symphony of their feelings.

Shame-Prone People Translate Criticism of What They Do into Judgment of What They Are

Shame-prone people hear a criticism of one thing they did wrong and feel as if their character had been called into question.

I once knew a much-loved minister who proudly subscribed to the theory that all human beings are by nature totally depraved, and it gave him special pride to admit that he was no exception. Now, you might think that a person who believed that his heart was rotten at the core would be more willing than most to accept some minor criticism of his behavior. I noticed, though, that whenever his wife reminded him of one small thing he forgot to do or had not done quite right, he took it as an assault against his worth as a human being.

"Dear," his wife might say, "you forgot to take out the trash this morning," or, if he had just come home from the supermarket, "Oh, dear, you bought margarine; what I needed was real butter."

Wounded by his wife's gentle rebuke, the minister wheeled his heavy guns into massive counterattack: "Why must you always put me down? I sacrifice myself to make life a little easier around here for you, and now, when you know I have a terrible headache, you cannot resist telling me what a miserable failure of a husband I am." He blankets his whole being with one criticism the way one ocean wave at high tide covers the whole beach.

Why does his wife's trivial criticism give him such needless grief? Here is my explanation: he is clobbering his wife with a rage he feels toward himself.

The fact is that this much-admired minister of God's love hates himself. Somewhere below the level of his good sense, he feels like a shamefully unworthy person. Yet he knows—in spite of what he feels—that he is, all things considered, a pretty good person. Thus, while one part of him hates himself, the other part hates himself for hating himself.

This man's shame is a bleeding ulcer waiting to be irritated. His wife obliges; she scuffs his shame with the rough edge of a trivial criticism. He snarls. He does not really mean to snarl at his wife, however;

he is howling at himself. The rage that shame sets off in some re-
spected people is like a field mine; it will smash anyone, friend or
foe, who trips on it.

Shame-Prone People Read Their Own Shame into Other People's Minds

Shame-prone people have a hunch that other people have the same
negative feelings about them that they feel about themselves, and
what they guess other persons are feeling about them becomes more
grist for their shame.

When Doris and I arrived in Amsterdam to do graduate studies, the
first thing we needed were some furnished rooms to live in. We did
not know the language; the dogs on the street knew more Dutch
words than we did, so we felt grateful when a friend named Henri
offered to help. Henri checked out the rooms for rent that were listed
at the university and then loaned me a bicycle and led me around the
city on a hunt for lodgings. He was my interpreter.

At our first stop, we looked at a room in the rear of a small third-
floor apartment. A widow, fiftyish, whose husband had died in a concentration camp, owned the apartment and lived in the front. Along
with her back room, she offered us the privilege of sharing her small
kitchen. But the room looked cramped and dark and airless to me, and
I was afraid that Doris would be depressed by it. I told Henri that I
did not think the room would suit us. Henri told the woman we
would not be renting it.

The woman looked at me, gravely, I thought, and she seemed sad.
Maybe hurt. I saw myself as I thought she was seeing me—an ugly
American with no sympathy for the suffering her people had gone
through in the war, gallivanting into Europe with my pockets full of
dollars expecting to rent a villa for practically nothing. I knew she
despised me.

The woman turned away from me and spoke seriously to Henri.
Henri translated: "Mevrouw says that she will be happy to give you
her large front room and that she will move to the back room herself.

She says that the Americans had done so much for the Dutch people that the very least she can do is give you her best room." I told her that I could not accept her generous offer and left with Henri, feeling doubly ashamed of myself.

Projection! Believing that whatever we feel about ourselves is what other people are feeling about us. It is what shame-bent people do, and doing it aids and abets their shame.

Shame-Prone People Doubt Their Shame but Act as if They Believed It

Most shamed persons have some reservations about their shame. Their common sense tells them that they are not as bad as they feel, and they are angry at themselves for feeling worse about themselves than they deserve.

Shame-prone people sometimes contradict their shame by succeeding just often enough to prove to themselves that they are better persons than their shame lets them feel. However, just when they succeed, their false self stings them again. Their belief in their unworthiness is revived, so they crash back into failure.

I once had a brilliant undergraduate student who earned very high grades in all of his courses during his first semester. In the second semester he came to the edge of failing. He repeated his near failure for three more semesters. Then he left school, enrolled somewhere else, and repeated the cycle there: a smashing success the first semester, a failure after that.

Why would a bright young person force himself to fail when he obviously had more than enough ability to succeed? He is caught in a shame trap. The lure that his parents held out to him was: we will approve of you if you succeed. The trap they set for him was: you are not worthy to succeed.

This young man was thus caught in a bind that forced him into a three-step failure sequence. First, he succeeded in order to win his parents' approval. Then he felt shame for having a success he was not worthy to have. Third, since he was unworthy of success, he felt obligated to fail the next time he tried. Now and then his doubts would come back, and he would succeed again, one more time, only once again to launch himself brilliantly into failure and into still more shame.

———————

In sum, we who suffer undeserved shame tend to fan the flame of shame that was lit in us by others. We do it with various forms of self-deception. The fact that we deceive our own selves does not make our lie any less a lie. Nor does the fact that our deception makes us feel humble turn the lie into truth. As C. S. Lewis remarks somewhere, if a splendid artist says he is a dabbler, he is not being humble, he is only being false.

Twelve

Escapes from Shame

Covered with ashes, tearing my hair, my face scored by clawing, but with piercing eyes, I stand before all human beings recapitulating my shames . . . and saying: "I was the lowest of the low." . . . However, I have a superiority in that I know it, and this gives me . . . the advantage . . . the more I accuse myself, the more I have a right to judge you.

ALBERT CAMUS

John Wilkes Booth believed in slavery, but he did not lift a finger to save it. The South had lost the war it fought to save slavery, and he had been too much of a coward to do anything for the cause. His cowardice shamed him. "I despise myself," he said and went out looking for a chance to escape his shame. The chance came when a British play called *My American Cousin* opened at Ford's Theater, and it was rumored that the president would attend. Abraham Lincoln was a sacrifice to shame.

Booth's villainy leads me to ask this question: are people ashamed because they do bad things, or do people do bad things because they are ashamed?

Most students of shame believe that people do bad things because of their shame. They show us the childhoods of the foremost villains of recent history: Hitler, for instance, and Saddam Hussein. Most every monster was a disowned child—abused or abandoned—or in some other cruel way made to feel unworthy and unwanted. They all did great evil to overcome their sense of unworth. Most shame-based people tend to escape their shame in evils of lesser scope, getting themselves addicted to cocaine and alcohol and the like. However, whether they massacre others or only ruin themselves, they all do shameful things to escape their shame.

As true as it is that shamed people do bad things to escape from their shame, it is just as true that shamed people escape their shame by doing good things.

I have an English boy in mind, a bright boy born to illustrious parents who left him in the lurch so that they could devote all their energies to pursuit of their ambitions and pleasures. His father was much too obsessed with his frenzied but failed career in Parliament to pay the boy any notice. His enchanting American mother turned seduction of the rich and powerful men of England into a profitable career. She wore diamonds on her neck, diamonds on her fingers, and diamonds in her hair but never noticed whether her little boy had any shoes to wear.

His parents sent the boy away to a second-rate boarding school, where term after lonely term he dangled near the bottom of his class. He pleaded with his parents to visit him the way other boys' folks did, but they never came. His father wrote him cruel letters now and then to complain about how ashamed he was to be stuck with a dolt for a son, but he never came to call.

When Christmastime came, the scholars were shooed off from school, and the boy was obliged to go home. Often when he got there the only sign of his parents was a note they left behind for him: "We've gone to the Continent for the holidays. Nanny will look after you." Happily for him, he had a nanny who tried to make up in her loving care for the unloving carelessness of his parents—but not quite.

The boy grew up believing that he was not worth loving and that he would have to earn love by superior achievements. His only chance to escape his painful shame was to do great things to prove he was not only a worthy but a great man in the bargain. Supported by his nanny and inspired by his Marlborough forebears, he launched himself into honor and glory. His name was Winston Spencer Churchill.

Here is another shame-based child who made a career of escaping his shame. This boy's mother exiled him for weeks on end, threw him out of the family circle, cold-shouldered him, did not speak to him or touch him, and then, as if on a whim, took him in again. Serial abandonment worked its shame on him. The boy was thoroughly persuaded that he was not worthy of being loved. He turned his life into a whirling, snorting, hand-crushing crusade to escape his shame by proving to the world that he was lovable and acceptable no matter what his mother thought. His name was Lyndon Baines Johnson.

You never know for sure in what direction shame will push a person. John Cheever, one of the finer writers of our time, wrote in his diary of "the contemptible smallness, the mediocrity of my work, the disorder of my days." He was ashamed of his writing, but he had to keep on writing to escape the shame it gave him. A reviewer of his journal comments, "Over the years, we see him writing in shame and self-hatred." Yet he persevered, escaping his shame by writing some of the more haunting paragraphs ever put on paper. God only knows how much of our literature was created in an author's flight from shame.

Far better had the great prime minister and the tragic president and the brilliant writer been moved to true or near greatness for better reasons than to escape a shame they did not deserve to suffer. However, the way they dealt with their shame at least illustrates this point: not all shamed people become monsters, child abusers, or alcoholics.

Sometimes they do. Bill Trinkut, for instance, a man who wanted to do the right thing as much as most people do, did bad things to both himself and his son Tom. Bill had a chronic case of undeserved shame, was infected with it by his alcoholic father. Like his father, he drank a lot to dull his shame. Instead of soothing his shame, however, his drinking compounded it; he was ashamed of being an alcoholic father as well as a failed son of an alcoholic father.

He tried to escape his shame the way his own father had tried to escape his. He would require Tom to be a star, do well for himself, and thus, by his son's success, he would prove to himself that he was a good father and escape his shame. So he let Tom know that he would never get his father's acceptance unless he did well enough to make his father proud. Bill's shame, however, scuttled his plan. The same shame that pushed him to nag Tom to succeed pushed him in other devious ways to convince Tom that he did not deserve to succeed and was doomed to be a failure like his father. Tom digested the shame message; he was convinced subliminally that he did not deserve to succeed and so he failed. The shame that drove Bill to demand that Tom succeed drove him to assure that Tom would fail.

So Bill felt still one more layer of shame—he added the shame his father gave him to the shame of having shamed his own son. He clutched his shame, wouldn't part with it for the world, and absolutely refused to be healed; his shame, after all, gave him the best excuse he could find for drinking.

The law of shame: the shame of the father is visited upon the son unto the third and fourth generation.

Let me tell you, too, about a devout and sober father, an immigrant, bewildered by the craziness of the new world and scared to death by the sight of his little girl becoming, too soon for him, a woman. Driven crazy by the feelings the sight of her aroused in him, he seared her spirit with his shame.

"You look like a whore," he would sneer. "Maybe you are a whore."

He went on and on, driven by his terror at what was happening inside of himself. His daughter soon felt that she must be the sort of girl her father said she was, and she spent the rest of her brief life in and out of the role he wrote for her. On her fortieth birthday, she ended her own life as a final effort to escape a shame she never deserved to feel.

Here is a paradox for you: some shamed people do shameful things to prove to themselves that they are not ashamed to be what they are ashamed of being. They act out their shame with a fury in the hope that if they flaunt their shame they will convince themselves that they deserve it.

Nastasia Philapovna was a wondrous beauty quite capable of driving a sober man mad in a single hour alone with her. She struts in and out of a placid Russian village, where she sends proper matrons into a moral fit. She arouses the dormant libido of old men. She runs off with younger men and leaves them in the lurch the next morning, laughing as they threaten to kill themselves for her love.

Only Prince Mishkin, the somewhat idiotic saint, whom she truly loves, sees what is going on inside of her. The truth is that buried beneath her fantastic behavior Nastasia Philapovna carries a ferocious, self-destroying shame from which she is desperate to escape. The prince is the hero of *The Idiot*, written over a century and a half ago, considerably before anyone is supposed to have known about the psychology of shame, by the Russian prophet Fyodor Dostoyevski.

When Nastasia was a child, homeless, abandoned, and utterly lost, she was taken in by a rich patron who abused her and then kept her about him the way he kept an icon that he now and then took off the shelf and fondled. He left her with a shame that burned her soul.

Mishkin sees the shame behind her wildness:

> Oh, don't cry shame upon her, don't throw stones at her! She has tortured herself too much from the consciousness of her undeserved shame. . . . She had an irresistible inner craving to do something shameful, so as to say to herself at once, "There, you've done something shameful again, so you're a degraded creature." . . . Do you know that in that continual consciousness of shame there is perhaps a sort of awful unnatural enjoyment for her, a sort of revenge on someone?

Nastasia escaped her shame in spectacular scandal. *Petty* scandalizers like Sam act out their shame in piddling delinquencies.

Sam was a half-baked reprobate in my parish who took pleasure out of coming to my office and spilling his banal depravities over my desk. He was a tedious sinner; he lacked courage to sin bravely and lacked imagination to sin with style. Much as he wanted to keep the congregation in shock, he did no better, finally, than bemuse them with his trivial pursuit of the illicit life. He would sit with me longer than I wanted to sit with him and tell me more about his grubby soul than I wanted to know. Why did Sam want so badly for me to believe that he was worse than the average stinker?

It takes no analyst to know. From the beginning, Sam's father had drilled into him that he was foul to the pit of his sin-bedeviled soul. He became a totally shame-based person, and he escaped his shame by taking pride in being God's most disgusting discard. I thought that Sam needed to shift into some positive perspectives on his life, so I offered him some, but he was not about to let me strip him of his pride in being such a shame. He clutched his beloved shame and waited for another chance to prove that he really was a rake to be proud of.

Acting out our shame is the most desperate way to escape it. Are not most young people who set the teeth of responsible adults on edge these days doing precisely this? Do you know of any young rebel who is not being driven crazy by his or her own self-hatred? Drug-driven young people of the inner city, welded together by a wish to die, if dying is what it takes to prove that they are acceptable to their gang. Wild adolescents of plush suburbs, spinning their bewildered parents into a vertigo of fear and shame. Are they not acting out their shame to prove to themselves that what they are ashamed of being is what they really want to be?

Timid people escape shame by the opposite route. They try to get around their shame by conforming to the letter of the rules of their religion. Nelva is a young woman I know who escapes her shame by obeying every precept of her tradition. This is fairly easy to do because her religion's rules are mainly negative; she could be a saint by sleeping her life away. In fact, she might prefer to escape by sleep were it not that she sometimes breaks the taboos in her dreams.

Kin to the conformists are the self-righteous who paste their own shame on other people. What compels them is their dread of the ogres that inhabit their souls. They know the ogres are there. They fear them as they fear the devil, so they project their own ogres on the screen of other people's lives. Then they condemn those other people for having the demons that they fear within themselves. They hope, of course, that they will feel better about themselves if they flail at other people. But they don't feel better; they only hate themselves the more.

In desperation, shame-driven celebrities sometimes act out their shame in a fashion that almost certainly will get them caught; then they weep for their sins in public and become celebrity penitents—all in the hope that their public tears will wash away their shame.

Now and then a person is so ashamed that she becomes another person to escape her shame. I do not claim to understand how multiple personalities are created, but I am sure they exist. It may happen with people whose life has become too monstrously shameful for them to accept as their own life. It may happen with people who have suffered shame as a result of evil other people have done to them (most often sexual abuse by parents). In either case, their only escape from their shame of it is into a person who is ignorant of the existence of their shameful self.

The proper self goes about her daily life like a proper citizen, a proper mother, often a proper Christian, utterly oblivious of what the other self, the stranger self, is doing or has done in her body. Oblivious, indeed, that her shameful self exists.

Then some chance encounter with reality may trigger a terrifying hunch of some mysterious link between her two selves. Possibly, over years of therapeutic labor, the proper self becomes conscious that she and the shameful stranger are one self. At that moment, the possibility may be created for a gradual healing.

Maybe the simplest way people escape from shame is to deny that it exists. That is, they deny whatever it is that makes them ashamed. It happens in families that conspire to keep a terrible secret from themselves.

For example, a mother knows that her husband is abusing her daughter, but she chooses not to know. What he is doing is so shameful that, in an instant so brief that she does not know it has passed, she denies what she knows before she catches herself in the act of knowing it. She corrupts her consciousness, lies to herself, and denies that she is lying—all in order to escape the shame of the horror that is happening inside her lovely family.

People invent many ways to escape their shame. None of them work. They only push the shame out of the front door of their feelings and let it in again through the back door. The better way to deal with shame is not to escape it but to heal it. It is about time that we began thinking about doing that.

Intermezzo:
A Little Parable

One sodden September day in the year 1871, in the melancholic village of Norre Vosburg on the bleakest coast of Jutland, Babette Hersant knocked at the door of a modest cottage where two sisters, Martina and Phillipa, lived. Babette had recently been the chef of the Chez Anglais, a grand restaurant in Paris, but had fled France after her husband and child had been murdered in the civil war. Martina and Phillipa carried on the mission of their late father, leading a sect of believers on their joyless journey through this valley of pain and sorrow.

Since their leader's death, the flock had become more quarrelsome and even more joyless than before, which made the work of the sisters increasingly hard. So when Babette appeared at their door and asked if she could work for them, they knew she had been blown to them by the wind of the Spirit.

"Stay with us," they said. Stay she did and became the servant of the servants of gentle misery.

They practiced a religion of benign denial. For instance, they believed that they could be fit for the meat and drink of the spirit only if they rejected all pleasure in the food of the flesh. So the sisters taught Babette how to soak a flat fish overnight and then boil it thoroughly the next day. How to soak hard bread in water mixed with ale, cook it for one hour, and serve it as hot ale-bread. That was the menu, all of it, day in and day out, with no relief even on the Sabbath.

Babette gratefully accepted her servant's life among the grave folk of Norre Vosburg. The only contact that she had in France was a cousin who, every year, for old time's sake, bought a lottery ticket registered in Babette's name. Some years had gone by when one day a letter arrived for Babette from Paris. It was an official notice that her ticket had won the lottery. With it came a certificate drawn on the Bank of Paris for ten thousand francs. A fortune!

Babette pondered for a time what she should do with her unexpected wealth. She finally decided that she would use it to give a gift to the faithful of Norre Vosburg. She would give them the one gift that she had to give, just as they had given her what they had to give. She would prepare them a feast.

Babette sent a list of her requirements to her cousin in Paris. Not long afterward two small boats arrived from France loaded with the provisions she had ordered for the feast: live squab, a huge living turtle, quail, partridge, pheasant, hams, beef, every fresh vegetable of the season, ingredients for the exquisite pastries for which she had been famous throughout Paris, herbs and spices and fine wines, along with porcelain and crystal. The feast would be served on the one-hundredth birthday of their revered spiritual leader.

The entire congregation was invited. Having heard of the unheard-of things that had arrived by boat, the people took counsel together as to what they should do. They decided that they would endure the feast for the sake of the memory of their master, but in loyalty to his teaching they swore to one another that they would not enjoy the eating of it.

And so, on the evening of the feast, the faithful came to the cottage, dressed in their best black, at the appointed hour. They sat down in silence at the elegant table that Babette had set for them, hands folded piously on their laps, all of them awed by the array of crystal and porcelain that had been brought from Paris. As each course of the banquet was served, they received it with no sign of delight, ate with heads down, spoke to each other only in pious phrases recalling how their late leader taught them they were unworthy of the plainest of victuals, and succeeded at the start in giving no hint that one bite or sip was giving them pleasure—but they did eat. They slurped her turtle soup; they wolfed down her delicate fowl; they sliced into her red meats; they nibbled her flaky pastry; and they even sipped her vintage wines, including a Veuve Clicquot of 1860.

As they supped, their spirits gradually mellowed, even against their wills, by the wonder of Babette's lavish gift. They were drawn by her grace to see that there was something here, after all, more to enjoy than endure. Their blushing pleasure in Babette's feast, so foreign and forbidden to them a few moments earlier, began to overflow as pleasure in one another.

The talk took on a lighter tone. There were some smiles between bites. A woman burped modestly; an elder looked up at her and said, "Hallelujah." Neighbors recalled how they had now and then mistreated each other in the past, and as soon as one mentioned it, the other forgave. After coffee was taken, the congregation left, feeling lighter than when they came. They walked home arm in arm, their slow plod turned almost to a skip, and they hummed together a light tune remembered from lighter days.

Babette's reckless grace had caught them off guard, melted their resistance, made them feel as if, perhaps, after all, in spite of their undeserving, they were worthy of even so fine a gift. Their discovery made them the more grateful. Joy trickled through the crevices of their spirits when, for a moment, they opened them to the grace of Babette's lavish gift.

After the feast, the sisters remarked to Babette that now that she had so much money, she would soon be returning to Paris.

"Oh, but no," said Babette, "I have no money. I cannot go back."

"No money? But the ten thousand francs?"

"All spent on the feast."

"All of it? On the feast? But it was too much for you to give!"

"Ah, but an artist is never poor."

I fancied that during the night an angel appeared to Babette and said to her, "Henceforth, let your name be Grace."

PART FOUR

Grace and the Healing of Our Shame

Thirteen

The Beginning of Our Healing

When we treat a man as he is, we make him worse than he is.
When we treat him as if he is already what he potentially
could be, we make him what he should be.

JOHANN GOETHE

The healing of our shame begins best, I am convinced, with a spiritual experience—to be more specific, a spiritual experience of grace. Grace is an unconventional alternative to three conventional remedies for our feelings of unworthiness and unacceptableness.

Conventional responses may vary some in detail, but they never steer far from these:

- Lowering our ideals to the level of our abilities to meet them.
- Making ourselves acceptable enough to satisfy the ideals we already have.
- Persuading ourselves that we are just fine the way we are.

I do not believe that we can heal our shame by these methods. I do not think they go deep enough. I do not think we can make them work. Let me explain why.

The first option has this fundamental flaw: it assumes that we can dilute our ideals whenever we find them a bother.

But can we? Am I able to lower my ideals of personal integrity whenever I feel bad about lying? Or can I decide that my ideal of keeping commitments to my family no longer holds whenever I want to be unfaithful? Most of us sense that we do not have the option of changing our ideals to match our performance.

What we can do is separate the ideal of our true self from the ideals of our false self. Are we letting secular culture create the ideals we live by? Are we handing ourselves over to graceless religion or unaccepting parents to define the self we must be in order to be acceptable? If we are, we are being shamed by false ideals of a false self.

It helps, too, to separate our ideals from our goals. The difference between ideals and goals is this: ideals are about the persons we ought to be; goals are about things we want to do. Get a master's degree in two years. Earn $50,000 a year within five years. Lose ten pounds in five months. Learn to use a computer. These are decent goals to work for, all of them. But we can trim our goals without lowering our ideals.

When we confuse goals we want to accomplish with the persons we want to be, we become candidates for deeper shame.

Now consider the second option: healing our shame by making ourselves acceptable. This is a cure that tends to increase the shame it is intended to heal.

For one thing, people who feel shame usually feel incapable of improving themselves; the heaviness shades into hopelessness. To tell these people to raise their achievement to match their ideals may be like telling a paraplegic that he should take long walks to get his legs in shape.

For another, we do not reduce our shame by moral exercise. The star moral achievers among us are often the most burdened by a feeling of their unworthiness. Getting rid of shame through moral accomplishment is the gambit of graceless religion. It feeds the shame we want to heal.

The third conventional solution is all we have left: convincing ourselves that we are already acceptable enough. Usually, we do this with self-congratulatory hype. Self-hypnosis is one method; we can recite self-esteem slogans, like mantras, every hour. However, it may be that if your brain tells your feelings that you are a terrific human being, your feelings may not be listening. Shame is usually too heavy to be ratcheted up by self-hypnosis.

These, in sum, are a few reasons why an unconventional remedy may be the place to begin. We need a radical approach that gets to the deeper, hidden issue of shame.

We approach the heart of the matter when we ask why shame is such a heavy load for the human spirit to carry. Why does it have such power to rob us of the joy of living? Why, in short, does it hurt so much to feel unacceptable?

There can be only one reason: feeling unacceptable incites a deep fear of not being accepted. Gerhart Piers, a psychoanalyst whose work (*Shame and Guilt*) pioneered the current psychological interest in shame, tells us that "behind the feeling of shame stands . . . fear of abandonment." Carl Schneider (author of *Shame, Guilt, Exposure*) agrees: "The underlying dynamic of . . . shame is the fear of rejection."

Of course! The webs of shame that entrap us are woven with tangled threads of fear—fear that we may be rejected by someone very important to us. In short, inside our shame broods the worst of all fears, a fear that is the sting of death itself, the fear of rejection.

This lands us feet first at one of the most important points of this entire book: *the experience of being accepted is the beginning of healing for the feeling of being unacceptable.*

Being accepted is the single most compelling need of our lives; no human being can be a friend of herself while at the edges of her consciousness she feels a persistent fear that she may not be accepted by others. Not accepted by what others? By anyone important to us who may size us up and find us wanting. Our parents, our colleagues and bosses, our friends, especially ourselves, and finally our Maker and Redeemer.

Our struggle with shame, then, leaves us with this critical question: are we stuck with our merciless illusion that we need to be acceptable before we can feel accepted? Is there an alternative to the shame-producing ideals of secular culture, graceless religion, and unaccepting parents?

There is. It is called grace. Grace is the beginning of our healing because it offers the one thing we need most: to be accepted without regard to whether we are acceptable. Grace stands for gift; it is the gift of being accepted before we become acceptable.

Before we go on, I must explain that grace is not some sort of cosmic featherbed we can all flop into when we feel heavy. Grace is really shorthand for God, who, to the amazement of any shamed person, is amazingly gracious.

Describing the reality of grace, however, is like explaining quantum physics in a paragraph or shrinking Beethoven's Ninth Symphony to the length of a sound byte. I will reduce the challenge somewhat by speaking only of our *experience* of grace. Not about theories or doctrines of atonement. Not even about what God had to suffer in order to get grace to us or what one must do or believe in order to get it. To put it crudely, I will not discuss the price of admission; I shall only try to describe what we experience once we get inside.

Most people who experience the grace of God at all experience it on one or more of four levels:

- We experience grace as *pardon:* we are forgiven for wrongs we have done. Pardoning grace is the answer to guilt.
- We experience grace as *acceptance:* we are reunited with God and our true selves, accepted, cradled, held, affirmed, and loved. Accepting grace is the answer to shame.
- We experience grace as *power:* it provides a spiritual energy to shed the heaviness of shame and, in the lightness of grace, move toward the true self God means us to be.
- We experience grace as *gratitude:* it gives us a sense for the gift of life, a sense of wonder and sometimes elation at the lavish generosity of God.

The experience of grace that I shall be talking about here is, for the most part, the experience of being accepted. I will begin with this as our foundation: *the surest cure for the feeling of being an unacceptable person is the discovery that we are accepted by the grace of One whose acceptance of us matters most.*

To experience grace is to recover our lost inner child. The heart of our inner child is trust. We lose our childhood when we feel that the persons we trusted to accept us do not accept us or that they may reject us if we do things that displease them. Shame cheats us of childhood. Grace gives it back to us.

The trusting child does not have a worry in the world about whether he is smart enough, or handsome enough, whether he has accomplished enough with his life, or been good enough to be acceptable to his parent. He trusts that the someone who holds him, warms him, feeds him, cradles him, and loves him will accept him again and always. Trust is the inner child we rediscover in an experience of grace.

Grace overcomes shame, not by uncovering an overlooked cache of excellence in ourselves but simply by accepting us, the whole of us, with no regard to our beauty or our ugliness, our virtue or our vices. We are accepted wholesale. Accepted with no possibility of being rejected. Accepted once and accepted forever. Accepted at the ultimate depth of our being. We are given what we have longed for in every nook and nuance of every relationship.

We are ready for grace when we are bone tired of our struggle to be worthy and acceptable. After we have tried too long to earn the approval of everyone important to us, we are ready for grace. When we are tired of trying to be the person somebody sometime convinced us we had to be, we are ready for grace. When we have given up all hope of ever being an acceptable human being, we may hear in our hearts the ultimate reassurance: we are accepted, accepted by grace.

We Should Understand, However, That Grace Turns Conventional Moral Wisdom on Its Head

Think of some of those unquestioned moral maxims that only the reckless dare deny: "Nothing is for nothing." "There's no such thing as a free lunch." "To each his due." *Quid pro quo.* In one magic moment of grace, we fly beyond all of these conventional maxims.

Grace Is Also Outlandish

A first experience of grace could feel as if we had landed in a world where two plus two might knock at our door and introduce herself as five or where, when a wrench falls out of our hand, it rises to the ceiling. There is a weightlessness about grace. It has the feel of a fairy tale; what makes it a very special fairy tale is that it is true.

Grace Is Also Morally Dangerous

To be accepted whether or not we deserve to be accepted has always been an outrage to careful and rigid moralists. To the ancient Pharisees, for instance, it looked like the most wicked bargain ever offered to a sucker full of shame. In their straight-line moral bookkeeping there were two kinds of people: people who are acceptable enough to be accepted and people who are not. If you are one of the second kind, too bad for you.

Graceless religion worries that grace will turn a spiritually homeless person into a freeloader. If you can be accepted without being acceptable, why try? It is a fair question.

The answer to the question could begin with a comparison. Who has the better crack at living an acceptable life? A child who is warmly accepted by his parents from the start? Or a child who was abandoned and left with a persuasive hunch that she was rejected because she did not deserve to be accepted?

To make my point, I want to tell two stories. One of them is the story of Racehoss Sample. The other is the story of C. Prescott McCaernish. Racehoss is a real man's real name. C. Prescott is a made-up name for a real person.

Racehoss was Big Emma's boy. Big Emma was a smashing prostitute who made a living by providing gambling and bootleg liquor along with the sex she sold in a shack near a railroad stop in middle Texas. Racehoss got in Big Emma's way, and she resented him for it from the start. She beat him whenever she was drunk, which was a good deal of the time, and made him know that he was less than worthless.

When he got to be eleven years old, Racehoss could not stand it anymore and took off; he ran away to nowhere special, riding the rails wherever they took him, riding them with bums and hoboes, and, along the way, becoming a creature of volcanic rage. The Second

World War broke out, and the army found him but soon found it could not tame him. He went AWOL every month or so, and each time he did, he got into a fight and was sent to jail for assault and battery. Finally, they sentenced him to thirty years in the Texas state penitentiary. Here he learned for sure that if you treat a person like an animal, he becomes one.

The worst punishment they had for untamed prisoners was confinement in the tomb. The tomb was actually a four- by-eight-foot basement cell with no windows and two solid-steel plates for a door, a solid slab of concrete for a bed, a missing slab in the floor to pass for a toilet—the stench lingering on from occupant to occupant—and absolute darkness. This is where they stuck a prisoner who forgot to grovel low enough to suit his white boss, locked him in there for twenty-eight days, with one cup of water and one biscuit a day, and one meal of mush every six days to keep him alive.

Racehoss spent a considerable amount of his time in the tomb. In the sixteenth year of his captivity, he contradicted one of the guards and was locked in again, but it was not the same this time. This time he was terrified as soon as they shoved him in. He heard a sound as of rushing water nearby, and he knew for sure it was going to seep in and drown him. He went crazy.

I . . . ran around the walls. Then rolled on the floor like a ball. . . . I mauled myself, scratching and tearing at my body. Slumped, exhausted on the slab, I covered my face with both hands and cried out, "Help me God!! Help meeeee!!" . . .

And then—

A ray of light between my fingers. Slowly uncovering my face, the whole cell was illuminated like a 40 watt bulb turned on. The soft light soothed me and I no longer was afraid. Engulfed by a presence, I felt it reassuring me. It comforted me . . . I breathed freely. I had never felt such well being, so good, in all my life. Safe. Loved.

The voice within talked through the pit of my belly. "You are not an animal. You are a human being." And "Don't you worry about a thing. But you must tell them about me."

After that, God was real. He found me in the abyss of the burning hell, uplifted and fed my hungry soul, and breathed new life into my nostrils.

When they let Racehoss out, they weighed him and noted that he had gained five pounds.

The way God came to the tomb for Racehoss Sample may not be God's normal route to the human soul. God did come to him, however, and what Racehoss experienced when God came was pure grace. The only message Racehoss got was the word he had ached to hear just once from Big Emma, and now he heard it from God: you are accepted.

What came of such easygoing grace, a grace that accepted a sinner and demanded nothing but that he tell people whom it was he met in the tomb? A good deal, actually.

Racehoss walked out of prison on January 12, 1972, at 9:45 in the morning with ten dollars in his pocket. Later on, he wrote his memoirs,[1] but we learn elsewhere that he was the first ex-convict ever to work out of the governor's office, the first to serve as a probation officer, and the first to serve on the staff of the State Bar of Texas as a division head. He was given the Liberty Bell Award and was named the Outstanding Crime Prevention Citizen of Texas in 1981. He received a full pardon and changed his name to Alfred Sample in 1976.

I take Racehoss Sample's story as an exhibition of the truth that grace becomes a positive power in a shamed person who is accepted by grace without regard to whether he is acceptable.

Now comes the story of C. Prescott McCaernish. He was the son of a minister of the gospel than whom no man could have been more acceptable. The message he heard from the beginning was: "Your father is a great man of God, and if you can be half the man he is, you will do well." He heard it from his mother and from everybody around him, and he never forgot.

So C. Prescott devoted himself to the kind of life that might make him acceptable in the eyes of God and his father. The first thing he needed was to feel a call to be a minister. He felt one. By the time he was forty-five, he stood, six feet of pulpit eloquence in a flowing blue gown, preaching three splendid sermons to more than two thousand splendid believers every Sunday morning.

Was he half the man his father was? To 95 percent of the people, he was more than the man his father was. What was wrong with the other 5 percent? He gave them more. And then some more. He was available to everybody. Need some counsel? He would make time. A daughter's wedding? He turned it into a pageant. A delegate to the national assembly? More than willing to go, run for high office if the call came. Boards to be on? What were evenings for?

But on the inside C. Prescott McCaernish was a frightened child ashamed that he would never be the acceptable man his father was. He found someone who had a talent for accepting unacceptable men; she nestled him, warmed him, excited him, and accepted him. She took him in; the congregation put him out.

Here lies C. Prescott McCaernish: a casualty of viral unacceptability syndrome. He had grace in the palm of his hand, but he could not close his fingers around it and take it to his lips. He worked in the atmosphere of grace and breathed the smog of shame.

Grace genuinely experienced is not really dangerous at all. What is dangerous is the wearisome, joy-killing heaviness of living without grace.

Fourteen

With Our Shadows

Within my earthly temple there's a crowd:
There's one of us that's humble, one that's proud,
There's one that's broken-hearted for his sins,
And one that unrepentant sits and grins.
There's one that loves his neighbor as himself,
And one that cares for naught but fame and self.
From such perplexing care I would be free
If I could once determine which is me.

UNKNOWN

Grace gives us courage to look at the messy mixture of shadow and light inside of our lives, be ashamed of some of what we see, and then accept the good news that God accepts us with our shadows and all the ogres who live inside of them.

None of us is one simple sort of person. What we are is a set of walking contradictions. Dostoyevski always got at the truth of our contradictions by putting them in their utter extremes. For instance, he said, "Here the shores meet, here all contradictions live side by side . . . a lofty mind begins from the ideal of the Madonna and ends with the ideal of Sodom . . . the devil struggles with God, and the field of battle is the human heart." One of his characters, Dmitri Karamazov, groaned that he had both Jezebel the harlot and Mary the virgin inside of him; life would be simpler, he thought, if he could only get rid of one of them.

But our inner lives are not partitioned like day and night, with pure light on one side of us and total darkness on the other. Mostly, our souls are shadowed places; we live at the border where our dark sides block our light and throw a shadow over our interior places. We are mixtures, not all light on one side and all dark on the other, but a mix of both, and we cannot always tell where our light ends and our shadow begins or where our shadow ends and our darkness begins. All of us are collections of odds and ends stitched together, patchwork, a moral hodgepodge. We are a snarled yarn of mindless drives, wayward desires, good intentions, and noble visions.

Not many of us have daily consort with Belial; we do most of our business with imps and goblins. And ogres. Ogres feel at home in the shadows. Ogres are neither demons nor angels; they are more like trolls than devils. Oh, ogres can be nuisance enough; they stomp on things that make people happy, and they kill other people's joy if they get a chance. But they are mostly retailers in mischief, not wholesalers in evil.

I know that our insides can become very dark, and I know that there are persons among us whose hearts are totally captive to the evil they do. Their entire inner being is corrupted; they not only do evil, they are evil. People of the lie. They are too far gone for shame. They are the shameless. Only a rebirth can give them back their shame.

However, I am writing for people who are still close enough to their true selves to feel shame, and especially for those whose shame is out of touch with their reality.

Many of us feel shame not for our too-badness but for our not-good-enoughness. Not measuring up to snuff hurts us more than when we violate a law. Here are some examples. I want good things for my friends, but I am not able to celebrate the way I should when they get the prizes while I plug along without anybody noticing. I do not want you to lose your job, but if one of us has to lose our job, I will be glad if it is not I. I do not have it in me to brutalize another human being, but I would not be plunged into grief if a certain pushy competitor suffered a streak of bruising bad luck or even dropped dead in his tracks. I am committed to telling the truth, but if I badly want something that you have plenty of and I could get it by cheating a tad without your noticing, I would not bet my pension on my honesty.

These are the sorts of vices that my ogres specialize in. They do not push me to murder and mayhem or to steal and plunder. Yet they are mean and ugly inclinations, and, given certain circumstances, they could push me into mean and ugly actions. They shame me with what I must admit is a healthy shame.

There are also lesser imps that play games with our humanity. We never seem to get all of our goals met, our chores finished, our duties done. We are mushy setups for charming crooks and pushovers for our own deceits. We talk too much, tend to make fools out of ourselves now and then, and give people the impression that we are rather woodenheaded. We dream at night about kinky sex with unpermitted partners, and we are not as wounded by other people's suffering as we should be. These are also the sort of failings that can give people a case of shame and leave them unsure of whether they deserve to feel the shame they feel.

Are these the traits of moral swine? Are they gaping rips in the fabric of our character? Or are they more like loose stitches? Is our shame healthy or unhealthy? We are not sure. But at the moment we accept the grace of God, the question is not decisive. The point is that the grace of God comes to us in our scrambled spiritual disorder, our mangled inner mass, and accepts us with all our unsorted clutter, accepts us with all our potential for doing real evil and all our fascinating flaws that make us such interesting people. He accepts us totally as the spiritual stew we are.

We are accepted in our most fantastic contradictions and our boring corruptions. Accepted with our roaring vices and our purring virtues. We are damaged masterpieces, stunted saints; there are ogres and angels in our basements that we can hardly tell apart and that we have not dared to face up to. For the whole shadowed self each one of us is, grace has one loving phrase: you are accepted. Accepted. Accepted. Accepted.

Grace heals our shame, at the beginning, not by taking all our shame away and not by separating the sheep of undeserved shame from the goats of deserved shame but by removing the one thing all our shame makes us fear the most: rejection. Nothing that could make us unacceptable will keep God from accepting us.

No one whose shame is healed by grace has any reason to suppose he or she will in this life ever be pure light. She may in the energy of grace become more of the true self she is meant to be. The inner shadows may get lighter. Some of her ogres may give way to her angels. However, she will never be so pure of heart that grace is not needed nor so poor of spirit that grace will not accept her.

Fifteen

_____

Singing "Amazing Grace" Without Feeling Like a Wretch

[God] adorned [his children] with so many honours as to render their condition not far inferior to divine and celestial glory.

JOHN CALVIN

When grace comes to us graciously, it heals. When grace is offered ungraciously, it shames. You can tell that grace is gracious if it makes you feel better for having it, feel lighter, and, when it comes down to it, feel like the worthy human being you are. The question is: are we accepted by grace only in spite of our unworthiness or are we also accepted precisely because we are worthy?

A grace that makes us feel worse for having it is an ungracious grace and therefore not really grace at all. If grace heals our shame, it must be a grace that tells us we are worthy to have it. We need, I believe, to recognize that we are accepted not only in spite of our undeserving but because of our worth.

Is it possible that we could be undeserving of grace and yet worthy of it? As I see myself, I look both undeserving and worthy, in different ways, at different levels, and at different times. So perhaps I am accepted by grace both in spite of my shadows and also because of a light inside of me that the darkness cannot put out.

- The "amazing grace that saved a *wretch* like me" may uncover a glory in our bosom that the wretch in us could not forever hide.

- When we feel like wretches saved by a grace we do not deserve, we may also discover a worth within that makes us worthy of the grace that saved us.

You have, I am sure, caught my sense of difference between being deserving and being worthy. Think of the difference this way. If I deserve some good thing that comes my way, it is because I *did* something to earn it. If I am worthy, it is because I *am* somebody of enormous value.

On Palm Sunday morning, April 9, 1865, General Robert E. Lee put on his finest dress uniform, mounted Traveller, and rode away from his tired and tattered troops to Appomatox, where he would surrender his beaten army to General Ulysses S. Grant. As Lee rode to meet his conqueror, he fully expected that his men would be herded like cattle into railroad cars and taken to a Union prison and that he, as their general, would be tried and executed as a disgraced traitor.

In the tidy living room of the home where the vanquished and the victor met, Lee asked Grant what his terms of surrender were to be. Grant told Lee that his men were free to take their horses with them and go back to their little farms and that Lee too was free to go home and create a new life. Lee offered Grant his sword; Grant refused it. Lee heaved a sigh; he came expecting to be humiliated, and he left with dignity and honor. As he watched General Lee mount Traveller and ride back to his troops, Grant took off his hat and saluted his defeated enemy. It was a gracious grace. And it deeply affected the defeated general: as long as he lived, Lee allowed no critical word of Grant to be spoken in his presence.

Grace graciously given honors our worth as it overlooks our undeserving.

I have certain qualities that I share with my fellow human beings—things about us all that our Creator prizes. I also have my own special ember glowing inside me and now and then my ember is fanned into a flame colored with my own special glory. My shared humanity and my unique flame make me, I believe, a creature worthy to be accepted by the grace of God.

There are any number of things I do not deserve. I do not deserve the Congressional Medal of Honor; I have never done anything notably heroic. Nor do I deserve the Nobel Peace Prize; I have done little to improve the odds on peace. As for the Cy Young Award, forget it; I cannot even throw a curve ball. I suppose I shall live and die without ever deserving most of the world's prizes. I certainly will never deserve the grace that saved a wretch like me.

Some of us, I am sure, are less deserving than others. I know this to be true mainly because I know people who are more deserving—in some real but imprecise way—than I am. Take my old friend Harry Boer. Harry is my candidate for the person least likely ever to be corrupted by power or money or sex. When it comes to sheer, basic integrity, I know he is more deserving than I am.

However, I feel *more* deserving than Nick (the Crow) Macramendo—a dapper thug from New York who murdered a slew of people, including friends of his, in cold blood just to please his mobster bosses and then, when he got into trouble, squealed on his bosses to save his skin.

From the upper gallery of divine perfection, the difference between Harry, Nick, and me may look too small to matter, but only a crabbed spirit would be blind to the difference there is. As William James said once, "There is very little difference between one [person] and another, but what little there is is very important."

Some people have sold off so much of their core humanity to meanness and deceit and brutality that they do not deserve much of anything. All of us have whittled it down far enough for us to know that we cannot look God eyeball to eyeball and say of his amazing grace, "I had it coming."

But let's talk of being worthy. My mother made huge sacrifices for me and I am still trying to come to terms with her heroic grace. Did I deserve it? I know for sure that I did not. Was I worthy of it? I believe I was. I was worthy of her sacrifice simply because she brought me into the world as a magnificent human being with my own potential to make something of myself. I was worthy of what she did for me, even though I did not deserve it.

What, then, about the grace of God? Do I deserve it? Am I worthy of it?

Nothing could answer these questions better than the parable of the prodigal son.

The prodigal son felt an itch for a life faster than the one working his father's farm could offer, and he figured he deserved it. So he asked for and received his rightful share of the family estate. Then he disowned his father and his family, left the farm in the lurch, went off to a far country, and spent his money on good wine and bad women. When he went through his last denarius, he—a Jew—ended up on a hog farm and got so hungry he salivated over the swill he fed the hogs. What he really swallowed was a dose of healthy shame.

So he gambled on his father's grace and headed back home. He did not expect much, but he had no alternative. When his father saw him coming, belly full of shame, the stately old man pulled up his robe above his knees and scrambled out to meet him.

The first thing the shamed prodigal said to his father was, "I don't feel worthy to be called a son; take me on as a hired hand. I'll make my bed in the barn." But his father embraced him, threw a neighborhood party, and took him back in the family as a beloved son.

The older brother was understandably miffed, and he told his father exactly how he felt. I imagine the conversation might have gone something like this:

"The rotten kid does not deserve this."

"I know."

"Well, then, if you know he does not deserve it, why do you throw a banquet for him? Why, for that matter, do you let him back in our family at all?"

"Ah, you are right, he does not deserve it. But if you only knew him as I know him, you would know he is worthy to be my son. That fellow he became for a while out in the far country was not his true self; it was a stranger, a false self. But now he has come back to find his true self. And that self is worthy to be my son."

So much for the parable. What about God and me? Am I worthy of the grace of God—the way the prodigal was worthy to be a son? My own experience of grace tells me that I am.

Grace does not make me feel less; it makes me feel more worthy. Even though it accepts me in spite of what I am, shadows and darkness, it also accepts me for what I am, a rather unique creature of rather unusual worth.

No matter who sings our folk hymn to grace—a choir of prisoners in the state penitentiary, folks down on their luck, the rejected and despised, or high-placed guests at a presidential breakfast—all of us feel less like wretches for singing it. When I sing "Amazing Grace," I feel a worth inside of me that tells me I am a better person than the wretch whom only grace could save. This is the sweet, sweet irony of the grace that saves a wretch like me: it is a most gracious grace that tells me I am worth it.

Sixteen

Places to Find Traces of Grace

When it comes, will it come without warning
Just as I'm picking my nose?
Will it knock on my door in the morning,
Or tread in the bus on my toes?
Will it come like a change in the weather?
Will its greeting be courteous or rough?
Will it alter my life altogether?
Or tell me the truth about Love?

W. H. AUDEN

On a television show where I did not expect to be asked any really serious questions, the host surprised me with this one: "Where do you usually meet God?" I blurted the first thing that shot through my head: "In my friends." Yes, come to think of it, I do meet the grace of God in my friends.

There is, of course, a critical difference between a friend and a friendly person. Friendly people smile at you as if you were a friend even when you are not. There's nothing wrong with friendly strangers; they lubricate the machinery of commerce, but we do well to remember that friendly people do not necessarily mean to be our friends.

I meet the grace of God in real friends, not in friendly strangers.

No question about it, the face of an accepting friend has traces of grace. Cal Bulthuis was my friend for a quarter of a century. A couple of years after I moved to California, when we were not seeing each other so often, his doctor called me up and told me that Cal had a killer cancer and if I wanted to talk with him I had better come quickly. So I flew to Grand Rapids, Michigan, the very next day and spent a week with him in the hospital.

The day before I left Cal, he drew on what little strength he had to call my attention to some flaws he had been noticing in me that had him worried. He pointed them out to me, one by one, and said he hoped I would work on them after he was gone. He hugged me and said we should have been more open with each other and been more emotional with each other, and I planted a kiss on his cheek. Then I left. He died a few days afterward. When I remember Cal's face, I see a trace of grace.

If you wonder where God's grace can be found, find yourself a critical friend. A friend who wants you to be as good a person as you can be, a friend who dares to confront your flaws and failures, and then accepts the whole of you in grace.

Another place to find a trace of grace is in grace-tipped memories. I once again call in my mother as witness. She was loyal to her shame to the end, but a pure heart can set a twist of grace even on the lip of shame. Oddly enough, grace can filter through memories of a shame-riddled parent.

My mother fed it to me in small bites. Mostly nights; she was away during the day except on Mondays and Tuesdays. On Mondays she stayed home to wash four or five families' worth of clothes in an un-cooperative secondhand Maytag—the old kind, with a wringer that you fed the clothes through before you put them in a tub of hot rinse water. I went down to the basement when I came home from school. Her dress was soaking wet; her hair, unstrung by steam, dangled over her forehead; her face was red; her back ached and, now and then, when she wasn't looking, she would get her hand caught in the wringer and give out a whoop of pain. All the while she kept a corner of her eye on the brass tub of water steaming alongside a black pot of brown beans on a coal-burning stove. Monday did not feel to me like grace day.

On Tuesdays, when I came home from school at noon, my mother was in the kitchen ironing the clothes she washed on Monday. She knew what she was doing in front of an ironing board, and she addressed it with aggressive confidence; a smoothly ironed shirt collar was her one pride in life. She would press sweet starch into one crumpled piece of cotton or linen after another. Wearing a dry cotton floral print house-dress under a plain gray apron, with her hair combed back in a bundle, she made me glad it was Tuesday instead of Monday. When I came home, she sat down beside me, and we ate lunch together, and she asked me how things had gone for me at school that morning. Tuesday was grace day, and it was a very lovely day.

My mother believed in holidays. They were all grace days. On the morning of Memorial Day we walked a few miles together to Oakwood cemetery, planted a little row of pansies, and stood for a while alongside my father's unmarked grave. On the morning of the Fourth of July she packed a basket full with bologna and peanut butter sandwiches, a bunch of bananas, two jars of lemonade, along with some square pieces of yellow cake. She traipsed with the five of us kids along the side of Getty Street, a busy road that had no sidewalk, pestering us to stay on the dirt apron out of harm's way until we got to the terminal of a streetcar line where we boarded a car for a day at two separate beaches, one at the big lake to watch a balloon ascension and, when evening came, the other at a small lake to watch fireworks that to me were a divine effulgence. Then we loaded ourselves on the streetcar again, and rode it back to Marquette and Getty.

On Christmas morning there was a spindly green tree in the living room that my mother went out to fetch on Christmas Eve at a give-away price a minute before the lot closed down. She made the tree glorious with glistening tinsel and a ribbon of red paper after we all had gone to bed. She stacked presents for all of us underneath it, mostly underwear and socks, but in the good years a doll, too, a ball, a puzzle, and once a mechanical marvel of a metal airplane with a high red wing and a propeller that was driven by a rubber band attached to the spindle that connected with its front wheels so that the propeller went around when I wheeled the airplane along the floor. Always there were black stockings full of navel oranges with thick peelings, balls of popcorn, and hard Christmas candy. Oh, my Lord, my Lord, how she did grace our holidays.

Once I sat under a mulberry tree with some bigger kids and tried to smoke some cigarette butts that they had picked up along the curb, but I became awfully dizzy and I sneaked home sick. It was a Tuesday, so my mother was there to take me in, which she did, and when she smelled what I had been up to, she said that any boy who got that sick from smoking needed an ice-cream cone to calm his stomach. She gave my older brother a nickel and shooed him off to the drug store to buy me one.

A year after I finished high school with anything but luster, and afraid that I lacked intelligence enough to succeed in college, I decided to follow my longing for learning and maybe even a call to the ministry at Moody Bible Institute in Chicago, where they took in candidates of lesser promise. The morning I left home, my mother walked with me the two miles it took to get downtown, where I caught a Greyhound bus for Chicago. She waited alongside until the bus backed out of its parking stall, and I saw tears flowing down her cheeks while she waved goodbye to me.

My mother lived out her days in the shaky house my father had almost finished making for her with his own unskilled hands after working hours before he died at thirty-one. Inner-city blight seeped into her neighborhood during the years after we kids had left, but she stayed there. She judged no one, indulged everyone, got to be known as the candy lady because she always had some candy for the kids, and in general worked a neighbor's magic with her grace.

She died a week after I saw her last, the time she told me what a great sinner she had been. We planned a modest little funeral for her, just the family and a few friends, about what we expected to come to say goodbye to an unknown widow who lived alone in a neighborhood where nobody she used to know lived anymore. However, more people than we knew had tasted her grace, and they came—white people, black people, neighbors of the time of decay and neighbors of the better days, church people and people who never went to church, very poor people and people who were well off, children and ancients-of-days, workers and bosses from the foundry whose offices she last kept clean—they came, a swarm of them, and they said they came because my mother had brought some lightness into their heavy lives.

Enough, I think, to establish the mystery that grace can make even shame its servant.

For grown-ups who did not find any traces of grace in their parents, the best bet is to find another sort of family, a community that is in the business of channeling the grace of God.

In Pulaski, Tennessee, where the Ku Klux Klan was born, a young minister named George Regas opened the door of his office one day to a woman who had scandalized the town by having a spectacular affair with a man who really stood for something in town. She did not have to tell the minister who she was: in Pulaski everybody knew her.

In public Amerelda—let's call her that—flaunted the furies of southern shame, and in high style, too. She had been kicked out of the Methodist church. Divorced by her husband. But she wore her scarlet letter with withering nonchalance.

However, in the office of the young minister Amerelda was a tired spirit heavy with shame: "Father Regas, I am not worthy of God, but I desperately need him. I'll do anything to gain back God's love. Help me. Help me, please. I'm so empty." He told her that there was nothing she could do to gain back God's love because she had never lost it.

Amerelda fought a savage fight against grace; her sin was too sordid, her character too soiled for grace. Regas countered, "No, no, that's not the way it works. God will accept you as you are. By his grace. You already feel all the sorrow you need to feel."

Amerelda gradually let herself be accepted by God and gradually accepted herself in the same grace God gave to her. She slowly let the unshaming acceptance of people in that church get inside her soul. In the feeling of their acceptance she felt the wonder word of God: you are accepted. I do not believe this shamed woman could have discovered the grace of God in Pulaski, Tennessee, if she had not met him in the faces of a family of grace-based persons.

After Amerelda's heavy shame had been replaced by the lightness of grace, she became a grace-embodying person for others. There, in Pulaski, in the year 1957, when the Ku Klux Klan set the moral agenda,

Amerelda reached out in grace to her black sisters and brothers, accepting them as she had been accepted. It is the law of grace.

Grace-based churches are not dispensing cheap grace. They call sinners to repentance, and they call saints to service. But they put grace up front, center stage, at the raising of the curtain and keep it there until the curtain falls.

Sometimes a person finds grace not in church but in her own internal tomb. In her own despair. Despair, like hell, is where we experience the absence of God. However, in the very place we feel most desolate, he can find us, and when he does, we will know for sure he comes with grace.

I am talking about the darkness that entombs us inside the feeling of our unworthiness. A shamed person can slide into this hell without realizing where he is headed. I have been there—and I have met grace there. If I scribble a feature or two about the experience, anyone who has been there will recognize the darkness I am talking about.

Mind you, I believed in God at the time, and with my head I believed in grace. I was not groveling in guilt with some horrendous sin stuck in my crop. I was feeling a load of unhealed shame that had little contact with my reality.

I felt all alone. Helpless. Drained. The ideals I had tried and failed to live up to were so absolute and so undefined that my shame was equally absolute and undefined. I was hopeless. I seemed to be sinking into a darkness where I would be stuck forever.

It was only a dark *feeling*, you say. But feeling *is* what hurts when it comes to shame. When a person with more unhealed shame than he can bear finally gives in to his feelings, he falls into a sadness that he has stored up and not dared to feel for years. It is a mourning for a lost joy. He is not sad *about* something in particular; the specifics are buried in events he cannot recall. It does not matter. What matters is that, finally, he is feeling it.

The sadness leads him gradually deeper into his darkness until he feels almost the full load of his shame, his fear that he is so unacceptable that no one can accept him—or should accept him.

It was there, at the bottom, that I discovered clear traces of grace. My desolation inexplicably gave way to comfort. I felt held and undergirded and accepted and loved. It was only afterward, as I thought about it, that I realized that what I had experienced was the grace of God. I had heard the word: you are accepted. My feelings echoed: I am accepted.

I heard no recordable voice. I felt no physical sensation. But I felt that I was accepted and would not be rejected, was held and would not fall, was loved and would never be unloved. I have since thought that I experienced what the psalm writer must have felt before he wrote: "If I make my bed in hell . . . even there shall your right hand hold me."

I want to tell you that the "dark night of the soul" is no spiritual tourist attraction. I recommend it to nobody. But if you do ever land there and feel the full weight of shame, that is where God may find you, and when he does, he will bring grace with him.

Grace is seen not in traces but full face in the story of Jesus. As I read the gospels, I am entranced by the simple and spontaneous way he accepted people heavy laden by their sense of being unacceptable. Accepted them, the publicans and sinners who were despised and rejected by those who thought they alone were acceptable, mired in the struggle nobody ever wins, the struggle to make themselves acceptable enough to be accepted by God. When he met them he would simply say, without looking up their credentials or investigating their pasts, your sins are forgiven, you are accepted, go in peace. No doubt about it, I meet the grace of God in the face of Jesus.

But where do I see the face of Jesus? Today, in my world, in the places I walk, among the people I know, where do I see traces of his grace?

I have found traces of grace in the faces of my friends, in the face of my mother, and in the faces of a community whose sole reason for existence is to convey grace to shamed people. At least once in my life, I found the clearest traces in my private desolation the way Racehoss Sample found grace in the tomb of the state penitentiary.

PART FIVE

The Lightness of Grace

Seventeen

Coming to Terms with Our Shamers

*The only possible redemption from the predicament of being unable to
undo what one has done . . . is the faculty of forgiving.*

HANNAH ARENDT

To be healed of shame we do not deserve, we must, sooner or later,
come to terms with our feelings about the person or persons who
shamed us. We who carry a shame that we do not deserve are likely
to feel a long-fermenting resentment of the person who infected us.
If we do not heal our resentment we can hinder the healing of our
shame.

How do we heal our resentment? One thing is absolute: the fact that
somebody shamed us is sculpted into our reality, and nobody can
chisel it out. We cannot undo what was done to us. We have been
wounded, and we carry our woundedness as part of our unchangeable
reality. The only reality we can alter is the reality of our feelings.
The question is: how can we change our feelings?

The way I recommend is the hard remedy of forgiving. It is, in
the end, the only remedy we have. None of the options to forgiving
does us any good. Revenge does not heal; it only makes things worse.
Forgetting does not help. If we think we have forgotten, we have
probably only stuffed the memory beneath our consciousness to fes-
ter there as the poisonous source of assorted other pains. Besides,
some things should never be forgotten. The only option we have left

is the creative act of forgiving our shamers with the same grace that enables us to forgive ourselves.

Forgiving is difficult; this is the first thing we need to know. The second is that the first and often the only person to be healed by forgiveness is the person who does the forgiving. The third thing we need to understand is what we actually do when we forgive someone.

Consider forgiveness as a personal drama with five scenes.

Scene One: We blame the shamer.
We hold him or her accountable. If we do not hold people accountable for what they did to us, we will not forgive them. We may indulge them, perhaps, as if it did not matter much, or we may excuse them, as if they could not help doing what they did. But we will forgive them only if we hold them responsible for what they did to us.

Scene Two: We surrender our right to get even.
We take our natural right to a balanced account—a right to fairness, mind you, that is all, only what we deserve—we take it in our hands, look it over, consider its possibilities, and then surrender it. We agree to live with the score untied.

Scene Three: We revise our caricature of the person who shamed us.
When we taste our resentment, we roll it around our minds the way we roll a sour lozenge around our tongues, and, as we taste it, our minds draw a caricature of our shamer. We turn him into a monster who *is* what he did to us. We see him; we feel him; we define his whole person in terms of how he shamed us. However, as we move with the forgiving flow, we gradually change our monster back into the weak and faulty human being he is (or was), not all that different from ourselves.

Scene Four: We revise our feelings.
As the frozen tundra of resentment melts, a tendril of compassion breaks through the crust. Sorrow blends with anger. Sympathy softens

resentment. We feel emerging in our consciousness a hesitant desire for the other person's welfare.

Scene Five: We accept the person who made us feel unacceptable.
In the last scene in the drama, we offer our shamer the grace that God has offered us. We not only pardon him; we also accept him. We take him back into our lives as a fellow member of the human family. Chances are that we are not able to restore the special relationship we had before. But if we cannot be reconciled, it will not be our resentment that prevents it.

Some Advice to Those Who Want to Forgive Their Shamers

Forgiving is delicate soul surgery. Botched surgery can be worse than no surgery, and botched forgiveness can be worse than no forgiveness. There are some common mistakes well-meaning forgivers easily make, and if we can avoid them we may spare ourselves some needless frustration. Let me offer some advice.

TRY UNDERSTANDING FIRST

Before we rush to forgiveness, we should explore understanding. If we understand that our parents simply could not help themselves, that they were powerless against their own shame, we do not blame them, and we do not forgive them. Our bitterness will wash out of our mind in the waters of compassion. We can understand some things, of course, make some allowances for our shamer's weaknesses, and still believe that he did not have to do them and not understand why he did; in that case, our only recourse is to blame and forgive.

SEPARATE WHAT YOU CAN PUT UP WITH FROM WHAT YOU NEED TO FORGIVE

Most of the pain we suffer from our parents is not the sort that needs to be forgiven. Parenting rambunctious children is a tough job for imperfect people. Good parents make bad mistakes. Oh, yes, they do lots of things wrong, but raising us was a job nobody could do exactly right. We were often a pain in their neck; we taxed their patience beyond any human being's breaking point. If our parents bungled their parenting now and then, they were doing what all imperfect people tend to do.

There is an underrated human quality called magnanimity, which literally means being a large soul, large enough to put up with imperfect people, and we should try it before we hurry to forgive.

DON'T BE HASTY

It has taken us a while to nourish a childhood misery into a life of adult shame. It may take a while to forgive the person who infected us. We should not expect to heal our shame with one flash of forgiveness. Forgiving works incrementally, like compound interest, and it is a long-term investment.

Quick-draw forgivers rush into forgiving before they know the lay of the land. They load forgiveness on people who do not need to be forgiven, or they forgive people too easily without holding them to account.

Worst of all, hasty forgivers often use forgiveness to get other people under their thumb. Henrik Ibsen saw it clearly in his play *A Doll's House*. A banker by the name of Torvald forgave his wife Nora. For what? What did she do? What Nora did was this: she had foolishly run up some debts and gotten herself into the kind of financial jam that an enemy could use to make a lot of trouble for her husband.

Nora had not told Torvald, but he found out. Seeing the mess he might be in, he went into a fierce rage. He confronted her. He would not divorce her, he said, he would keep her around where he could remind her every day that he hated her. He would keep her in the house, but he would not allow her to be a mother to their children.

Almost as soon as he had condemned Nora to the status of a possession, Torvald learned that the terrible secret would be kept and his career was saved. He forgave her instantly. "It is true, Nora, I swear it; I have forgiven you everything. . . . There is something so indescribably sweet and satisfying to a man in the knowledge that he has forgiven his wife. . . ."

What made forgiving so sweet to him? It was sweet to him because it gave him total control over her. She owed him everything. Ibsen explains: "It . . . made her, as it were, doubly his [possession]. . . . She has in a way become both wife and child to him."

Make no mistake. Hasty forgiving can be the meanest trick of all.

DON'T WAIT TOO LONG

If we wait too long, our resentment seeps into the pores of our personality. It assumes our identity. Our resentment becomes less what we feel than what we are. It possesses so much of us that surrendering it means tearing away a segment of our own self.

I once persuaded a church to admit its fault for unfairly firing and, in the process, shaming its minister. With a rare grace, this congregation confessed the wrong it did to him and pleaded with him to forgive them.

Well and good, but the congregation had waited thirty years. During those three decades, the minister's rage had become a part of who he was: "I have had my anger for so long, I won't know myself without it." But he began to forgive and began to rediscover his true self again.

BE CONCRETE

We should forgive in verbs, not in nouns. Forgive people for what they *do*, not for what they *are*. Retail forgiving is for us, not wholesale. It is hard enough to forgive anyone for doing a bad thing; it is almost impossible to forgive someone for being a bad person. Not even God forgives us for what we are. He forgives us for what we do and then accepts us for what we are.

DO NOT WAIT FOR YOUR SHAMER TO REPENT

Our shamer would make it much easier to forgive him if he would crawl to us in sackcloth and ashes. But if we wait for him to grovel at our feet, we may wait forever. If we keep waiting for him to tell us he is sorry, we put our own healing in the hands of someone who may never get around to saying it. So, in the worst of ironies, we give the person who shamed us the power to prevent us from healing the very shame he caused.

DO NOT FORGIVE OUT OF A SENSE OF DUTY

I cannot prove it, but I am sure that no one has ever forgiven another human being out of duty. Remember that God was not obligated to forgive. He forgives us only because he wants to. We too will forgive only when we want to forgive, or at least when we want to want to forgive. If we get that far, grace will take us the rest of the way.

BEGIN BY PRETENDING IF YOU NEED TO

Prime the pump by acting as if you are forgiving. There is only a very thin line between pretending to do something and actually beginning to do it. We can begin by thinking forgiving thoughts when we do not yet feel them and by saying forgiving words when we do not yet intend them. The thinking and the saying will be prime for the dry soul, and we may cross the line between pretending and doing before we know we have come to it.

SETTLE FOR SILENT FORGIVING IF YOU MUST

The ideal script calls for the forgiver to go to the shamer and say, "I forgive you," but it is not always a good idea to do that. Not everyone has the knack of saying good things well. If we do not say it in the right way or at the right time or for the right reason, we may do more harm than if we did not say it at all. Besides, the person you forgive may not be ready to hear you. In fact, he may never forgive you for forgiving him, and then where will you be?

Sometimes we can be satisfied to do the work of forgiving and leave the words for later when the time is ripe for words. When the time comes, we may not need words.

―――――――――

One of my favorite persons is a powerful and beautiful woman who spent half her life believing that she was weak and ugly. When she was growing up, she thought her father was a spitting image of the Lord God Almighty. When her god abused her, she tried to believe that she must have deserved it. Only when she began feeling the power to trust that she was being accepted by grace did she dare blame her father for what he did.

The *coup de grace* came when her hatred erupted through the crust of her fears. She screamed to her father, who was two thousand miles away, "I hate you, I hate you. You are the Devil; you are a monster. I hate you." With that, she got through the first scene in the drama of forgiveness.

This woman was lucky. Her father was honest—and penitent. She is plodding through forgiveness with him, well on the way to healing. Forgiving is a journey, sometimes a long one, and we may need some time before we get to the station of complete healing, but the nice thing is that we are being healed en route.

When we genuinely forgive, we set a prisoner free and then discover that the prisoner we set free was us. We walk in grace and gradually learn to dance.

Eighteen

Accepting Ourselves

[This is] . . . the categorical imperative of the Christian faith:
You shall lovingly accept the humanity entrusted to you! . . .
You shall embrace yourself.

JOHANNES METZ

To experience acceptance is the beginning of our healing; to accept ourselves is a signal that we are getting healthy. We all want to accept ourselves as badly as we want to be accepted. But what does self-acceptance really come to? What are we supposed to be doing when we finally accept ourselves?

First We Need to See That Accepting Ourselves Is Not the Same as Forgiving Ourselves

We forgive ourselves for things we *did.* We accept ourselves as the persons we *are.* When we forgive ourselves, we heal our guilt; when we accept ourselves, we heal our shame. Forgiving ourselves is spade work we do on the way to accepting ourselves.

When we forgive ourselves, we do essentially the same thing we do when we forgive another person.

- We hold ourselves accountable for what we did.
- We surrender our need to punish ourselves.
- We revise our understanding of ourselves; we are weak and faulty persons, so we can have compassion for ourselves to balance our judgment of ourselves.

- We revise our feelings about ourselves; we are responsible persons who fail, but we are also worthy persons who are accepted by grace.
- We make a move toward reconciliation with ourselves or, in other words, toward accepting ourselves.

From this sketch, we can see that self-forgiveness paves the road to self-acceptance. We are ready, then, to go on with the task at hand: accepting ourselves.

I tend to think of accepting myself as taking ownership of myself. Ownership puts some muscle on what is otherwise a flabby sort of word. It hints that there is more to accepting ourselves than feeling good about ourselves. When we take ownership of the person we are, we take on a full-time job.

I am going to suggest four ways that lead to ownership of ourselves.

- We own our raw material; we take responsibility for building a life out of whatever raw materials we have been given.
- We own the shadowy self beneath the surface of the self that is open to the public.
- We take pride in the self we own.
- We feel some joy in the self we own—a matter so important that I will reserve it for the final chapter.

Before we explore these four ways to self-ownership, let me remind you of which self we want to own.

I have, here and there, identified three selves: our true self, our false self, and our actual self.

Our true self is the self we are meant by our Maker to be. Our false self is the fabricated self that other people require us to be. But the self that grace permits and enables us to accept is the actual self that we are here and now, in the ordinary, sometimes grubby, often painful day we are blessed to be alive in.

Our actual self exists on two levels:

- the visible level: the past and the present chapters of the stories we are writing with our lives

- the deeper level: our depths where stir our conflicting motives and aspirations, our drives and inclinations, along with all that is buried in our subconscious selves

The healing of our shame is accomplished as we own our actual selves on both levels.

Now let's get on with the four ways to self-ownership.

We Own Our Raw Material

Our genetic bank account provides us with the basic raw materials for building a life. We were handed a set of genetic building blocks, the only set we shall ever get, and there we were, take it or leave it. Then we were given the family setting where our stories had to begin. We were plunked into it without being given a veto. The rest was up to us.

Some of us were given the unfair advantage of superior genes, and then were also bathed in an atmosphere of affirming family love. Others of us were shortchanged on both: we inherited a genetic deficit and choked on the foul breath of family abuse. Most of us were given a mixture.

The raw materials we get may put us at an unfair disadvantage. Take my son, John, for instance. Two people saw to his raw material in one act of careless love; at the crest of their passion they launched him into existence, and, while they were at it, they stuck him with a rare genetic and, to this point, incurable blood disease. They had one chance in ten million to pass it on, but they beat the odds without even trying.

Then, before John was born, his birth mother gave him to us for his family setting. We provided his setting: we gave him his place, his name, his family, his religion, his moral environment, and our love. He had not a whisper, let alone a voice, in selecting either his genetic raw material or his family setting.

For John to own himself, he had to begin with owning the only raw material he is ever going to get. Having owned that raw material, he is building himself a good life.

My own raw material gave me one advantage. It was my providence to be born the last of five children. When I came, my father died, and that was that. My oldest brother and sister, every bit as gifted as I and maybe more deserving, had to leave school early—my sister after only eight grades—and get whatever work was available during the great depression to make some money for themselves and to help put something on the table for me.

When I grew up, there were no young ones for me to be responsible for. I had a chance to fumble my way into higher education, a privilege with fringe benefits that keep falling in my lap to this day—all mine simply because I was born last instead of first. They were the raw materials I was given, and, as John has to accept his raw materials with courage, I need to accept mine with gratitude. Each of us can only do what we can with what we have been given to do it with.

Once in a while, later on, we may be pressed into a setting by forces beyond our control, evil forces possibly, and then, too, we have to decide whether we shall own ourselves within a life setting we would not have chosen. Now and then a person owns herself with so much grace that she mesmerizes the rest of us.

Etty Hillesum was one such person. Etty was a young Jewish woman, just twenty-seven, proud of her Jewishness, in love with God, and intoxicated with the gospels. Like all the others, she was caught in the circle of death drawn by the Nazis around Amsterdam in the Holland of 1941–45. Etty decided not to go into hiding; she did not want to escape the destiny of her family and friends. But she had to wait. While she waited for the day they would shove her into a boxcar and haul her off to Auschwitz, she came to terms with herself, with her inner self, and with her setting.

Etty was riding her bicycle on a Tuesday in November 1941 and talking to God: "I shall accept all the inevitable tumult and struggle. . . . I shall follow wherever Your hand leads me. . . . I shall allow myself to be perplexed time and again perhaps, in order to arrive at great certainty."

As the ring of extermination grew tighter in 1942, Etty did become certain:

> Very well then, this new certainty, that what they are after is our total destruction, I accept it. . . . Living and dying, sorrow and joy, the blisters on my feet and jasmine behind the house, the persecution, the unspeakable horrors—it is all as one in me and I accept it all . . . I have come

to terms with life. . . . And the funny thing is, I don't feel I'm in their clutches anyway . . . I don't feel in anybody's clutches; I feel safe in God's arms, to put it rhetorically, and . . . I shall always be able to stand on my own two feet even when they are planted on the hardest soil of the harshest reality.

I grant you that this is owning one's self on a dimension close to sublime: the more Etty owned her setting, the less she felt a prisoner of it. Then I remind myself that Etty was a passionate, erotic young woman. She fought her own demons and decided to live her inner life to the utmost, inside the gates of horror. She owned her life, her wondrous life within the only setting she had to live it in, and she owned it by accepting it as a gift from God. She owned her life even as they dragged her away and killed her in Auschwitz on the thirtieth of November in 1943.[1]

Grace does not permit us to waste our energies raging against the fates or the providence that dealt us raw materials we would like to trade in for a better set and stuck us in a setting we are not glad to be part of. Grace does not make it easy to accept the unacceptable raw materials or the tragic settings for our stories, but, if we can believe the Etty Hillesums of the world, grace makes it possible.

We Acknowledge Our Depths

We talked earlier about grace as God's acceptance of our whole menagerie of a self. Now I want to talk about grace as the power we are given to own our own darksome, sometimes threatening depths.

Mind you, we do not have to feel good about the shabby things that go on there, but we do have to acknowledge them, own them, respect them as part of the selves we are. Grace gives us permission: if God accepts us whole, light, dark, and shadowed, he gives us permission to accept ourselves whole.

In our depths we stuff sadness and joys we dared not feel. Our deep self pushes and pulls our surface self in directions that our surface self fears to go: a desire to strangle your father, a dark wish that one's mother-in-law would die, an urge to knock the boss's block off, a yen for forbidden sexual adventure, a longing to run away from the people we feel responsible for, or a yearning to die. All of these inclinations come from a real part of the real us. It takes a good bit of grace to accept them as ours.

There are also some splendid parts of ourselves down there that some of us are pained to own. There are a host of soft and tender angels that we keep submerged in our depths. Feelings, for instance. Feelings about what? Who knows. About almost anything. Gentle feelings. Romantic feelings. Hurt feelings. Feelings that could explode into ecstasy. Feelings that could set loose a tide of tears. Many of us have pressed our feelings down beneath the surface the way trash compactors compress our garbage behind our kitchen cupboards.

We are afraid our hearts may break. We fear we may lose control if we let our deep feelings break loose into our consciousness. But we cannot shoo our shadows away by denying them; they tag along with us like the tail on a lizard. And, oh, what joy and pain and integrity come when we give ourselves permission to own them as us.

Grace-based people dare to own any current, any drive, any sadness, any joy, any urge that might show up in their spiritual basements. They know that nothing in their conscious or unconscious selves can make them unacceptable to God. Grace makes self-knowledge bearable.

Do not forget that by owning our depths, we also free beautiful parts of ourselves that we have denied—free them to come out into the light, where we can relish them and thank God for them.

We Own Our Pride

Shame and pride are opposite feelings about ourselves. Shame—the feeling of being unworthy and unacceptable—is the loss of pride. As shame is healed, we find our pride again.

My mother could abide no pride. She could not abide it in poor people with big ideas or in rich people with big heads. She could not abide it in the proud way some people walk.

When I arrived in high school, I was a skinny rail taller than six feet. I usually drooped into a slouch to make myself an inch shorter than the lank spindle I was. My speech teacher noticed me one day and took me aside. "Lewis," she said, her eyes climbing up to meet mine, "you are lucky to be tall. Walk straight; be proud of your height." I dropped my slouch and slipped into a strut on the spot. When I strutted home my mother caught me at it: "Oh, Lewis, Lewis, Lewis, you must not walk so proud."

What my mother had against pride was that humility was safer.

> He that is down need fear no fall,
> He that is low no pride.
> He that is humble ever shall
> Have God to be his guide.

John Bunyan's pious poem expresses my mother's sentiments exactly. Better to stay down low where there is no place beneath to fall to. Her fear of pride was the tremor of her shame. It also happened to echo Christian teaching according to which pride is the worst of the seven deadly sins and the beginning of *all* our troubles.

Yet I am eager to tell you that the amazing grace that saves wretches like me encourages us to be proud. How come? This is how come: the pride that comes after grace is a very different thing than the pride that comes before the fall.

The pride that comes before the fall is what the Greeks called *hubris*. We call it arrogance. It is what my mother meant by the big head. "Undue self-exaltation" is what St. Augustine called it—self-esteem gone wild. Locate the haughty, the disdainful, the cocky, the know-it-alls, the white-collar crooks who clutter your life, and you have found yourself some people with hubris.

Hubris comes in three basic models: pride of power, pride of knowledge, and pride of virtue.

- A person with pride of power believes that his power itself gives him the right to do anything with his power that he gets into his head to do.
- A person with pride of knowledge believes that he has the whole truth and nothing but the truth in his head and that anything that contradicts his truth is a lie.
- A person with pride of virtue believes that he is God's model of virtue and that anybody whose way of life does not match his is probably living in sin.

Oddly enough, hubris is often born of shame. Shame-prone people are tempted to overcompensate by pretending that they are not only acceptable but also more acceptable than anyone else. But, as Reinhold Niebuhr taught us, the arrogant person never fully believes his own lies. He doubts his own pride, and the more he doubts, the more he struts his arrogant stuff.

There is, however, a healthy pride that comes with grace. A person who has experienced grace knows that what she is and what she has are gifts of God, so when she feels pride, she feels gratitude with the same impulse. We could put the difference between graceless arrogance and grace-based pride this way: arrogance is pride without gratitude, while grace-given pride is nothing but gratitude. A person with hubris thinks he is God. A person with grace-based pride thanks his God.

Grace-based pride is a kind of elation, especially about something we have accomplished. When we feel elation, we simply must share it; we have to show somebody what we have done so they can share our pride.

I see it in a child who has just tied her shoestring for the first time or turned a somersault: "Mommy, Mommy, look! Watch me. No, Mother, stop talking and come look." She feels what I suppose the Creator felt after he had made himself a fine world. When he saw how well he had done, he created some people who could share the world he was so proud of having made. Excellence cries for applause.

We also feel a pride in our own hearts when we share in someone else's achievement. It is the special pride of parents and teachers. It is like the pride of a father poking his neighbor in the ribs, jumping up and yelling, "That's my boy. That's *my* boy!" when his son hits a long fly ball to right field, or the pride of a teacher who sings hymns at heaven's gate when his deaf pupil first says his own name.

My friend Neil Warren once told me about how proud he felt as a small boy when he watched his father lead the congregation in the singing of gospel hymns. The sight of his father swinging both his arms with magisterial authority, urging the faithful to raise their voices to the praise of God, enraptured him. One Sunday little Neil's pride grabbed hold of him, pulled him away from his mother in the pew, and led him straight to the platform. He jumped up on it and stood beaming alongside his father in front of the whole church as if to say, "This great man is *my* father." He stretched his left arm around his father's thigh and pumped his right arm in authoritative circles the way his father did, only a half beat behind, ecstatic with shared pride.

Another graceful pride comes from accepting our share in the glory of something bigger and better than we are—a cause, maybe, or a family, or a nation. Paul the Apostle felt it when he gloried in the gospel and expected others to be proud of him for the way he proclaimed it to the world.[2] When Hitler tried to shame the Jews by forcing them to wear a yellow Star of David on their sleeves, one man in Amsterdam sewed a huge gold star on the front of his sweater, sucked in his belly and stuck out his chest, and strutted chin up past the German soldiers.

To complete this chapter, I will say only that as we gain the freedom to accept ourselves, we can be reasonably sure that we are healed of shame. Accepting ourselves is difficult. It is not a one-shot cure. It is rather like a long and wonderful passage. We accept ourselves when we take responsibility for writing our life stories out of whatever raw material we were given. We do it when we own the depths of ourselves even when what is going on down there scares us some. We do it when we take a grateful pride in what we do with our lives, in snippets or in full cloth. These are the makings of self-acceptance. They are warm-ups for the appearance of joy.

Nineteen

Living Life Lightly

*I must have clarity and I must learn to accept myself. Everything feels
so heavy inside me and I want so much to feel light. . . . I am a
happy person and I hold life dear indeed, in the year of our
Lord 1942, the umpteenth year of the war.*

ETTY HILLESUM

Shame is heavy; grace is light. Shame and grace are the two coun-
terforces in the human spirit: shame depresses; grace lifts. Shame is
like gravity, a psychic force that pulls us down. Grace is like levitation,
a spiritual force that defies gravity. If our spiritual experience does
not lighten our life, we are not experiencing grace.

Grace lightens our life at several points. I invite you to consider a
few of them with me in this chapter.

Living Lightly with Our Unhealthy Shame

Unhealthy shame—the shame we do not deserve to feel—attacks us
from the false self that passes as our true self. Our false self, recall, is
the self we strive to be in order to be acceptable to our secular culture, our graceless religion, or our unaccepting parents. Since the
self attacking us is false, its messages are also false. If we go on con-
fusing the self God means us to be with the self other people expect
us to be, we will go on and on with a load of unhealthy shame that has
no basis in reality.

Grace is our ultimate assurance that our false self has no validity and its message of shame has no threat. We can disclaim it with one sentence: I am accepted by grace. We can reject it. We can refuse to listen to it. We can cleanse ourselves of its influence forever.

Unhealthy shame is like a hard shell that we need to crack in order to find the beauty within us. It also keeps us from owning the shadowy and ugly things inside of us. Grace gives us courage to pry open the shell and look at both the beauty and the beast within.

Once we know we cannot be so unacceptable as to be unaccepted, we lose the fear of rejection by those who inflicted us with our unhealthy shame. We dare to track down the sources of our false shame, follow the trail even if it leads to the sacred doorsteps of our parents. We can name them, possibly forgive them, but certainly declare our freedom from them. We can look them full in the face and then be glad to know they can never again threaten us with the rejection we have needlessly feared for most of our lives.

We may need professional help to trace our false shame back to our shamers. We may need help to get rid of our false shame once we know where it came from. But daring to face up to our shamers and to open our eyes to the falseness of the shame they gave us is a first step in getting free from the shame we do not deserve. That courage has its source in amazing grace.

Living Lightly with Our Healthy Shame

Healthy shame, remember, is the call of our true selves. It is the price we pay for being persons who are really meant to be better persons than we actually are. It is also a signal that we are still close enough to our better selves to feel the pain of separation.

To be immune to shame is to have lost the better part of our humanity. The effect of grace is not to eliminate healthy shame but to eliminate its threat. The threat is the possibility of being rejected. Once grace cancels that possibility, the pain of shame is easier to bear.

Let me try a comparison. Imagine that you knew with absolute medical certainty that you were totally immune to cancer in any form.

If you knew that cancer could not invade your cells, you would dare feel pain in your stomach, pain in your bones, pain anywhere in your body because you are free from the threat of dying a slow death from cancer. Your immunity to cancer would not take away pain. But if you were absolutely certain that you could not get cancer of any kind, not if you tried, you could, with a light heart, seek the cause of your pain and find a way to heal it.

Grace is to healthy shame what immunity from cancer would be to physical pain. Shame is always painful, but grace extracts the threat of rejection just as immunity from cancer would eliminate the threat of death. In this way, grace gives us power to live lightly with a healthy shame none of us should ever wholly be without.

Living Lightly with Our True Selves

The grace-based person owns her better self as the self she is meant to be even though from one day to the next she falls several pegs short of it.

In a Christian experience of grace, a person even dares to own Christ as her true inner self. St. Paul did: "It is no longer I who live," said he, "but Christ who lives in me."[1] He traded the false self of religious conformity for the spiritual presence of the Christ within him and dared to claim that inner presence as his true self.

Delusion? I do not think so. Risky, yes; in a sickly mind, it could become a grandiose fantasy. But when St. Paul said that Christ was his true self, he meant that Jesus was the model of the self that he, Paul, never actually matched.

It takes courage to identify the Christ self as our own true self, because doing so could increase our shame for not living up to it. But while we do feel shame for failing to measure up to the level of our Christ self, grace emits waves of spiritual energy. First, the energy of trust: we will trust that the gap between our actual self and our Christ self will never be cause for rejection. Then the energy of hope: the Christ self we own as our true self is the self we can become. These currents of spiritual power free us and push us millimeter by millimeter as we sputter and stall on the way toward our true self.

Living Lightly with Our Imperfection

A friend of mine tells his wife that she is a model of perfect imperfection. He has a fine sense for the virtue of imperfection.

Imperfection is the mark of a good person who is capable of being even better. To feel our imperfection is to feel the energy of our potential—the push from what we are toward what we have it in us to be. Imperfection is not the wage of sin; it is the gift of our finitude, as being a bud before becoming a flower is the gift of nature's leisure.

Remember Stan Musial? Not many students of baseball would argue with the claim that he was the greatest outfielder ever to put on the uniform of a St. Louis Cardinal. Musial had the potential to get a hit every time he came to bat. He had it in him all right, but he did not do it. In his career, he failed to do his job around seven thousand times. And he succeeded only about three thousand times. In short, he failed two-thirds of the time. For a major league baseball player, this amounts to almost perfect imperfection.

Grace-based people live lightly with their imperfections because they see their imperfections as reason to be grateful and are thankful to be limited creatures with unlimited potential.

Living Lightly with Our Critics

Everybody wants a good review from her critics. Grace does not turn us into emotional pachyderms with hide so thick no negative critics can get inside. What grace gives us is freedom from addiction to their approval and the power not to be ashamed when we fail to get it.

Critics are a terror to people with unhealthy shame. There are so many of them—our mothers (who are alive and well in our heads long after they die), our children, our teachers, our colleagues—swarms of critics, and unhealthy shame creates a lust for rave reviews from each one of them.

Grace-based people take their critics lightly.

There is a passage in the New Testament that illustrates how it can be done. Some critics in the Greek city of Corinth threatened to shame the apostle Paul, and he put them on notice that he was not going to let them do it.

Here is what he said:

I've got a job to do, and what is asked of me is that I do it as faithfully as I can. What I am not required to do is please you. So what you—or anyone else for that matter—thinks about the way I am doing my job does not matter much to me. In fact, I do not even take my own criticisms very seriously. The only thing that really matters is what the Lord thinks about what I do and how I do it.[2]

I like that, and this is what I like about it: the apostle did not put himself above criticism. He only said that he was beyond being shamed by his critics.

About ten years ago, I decided to make a change in my vocation. I was teaching at a school that expected its teachers to produce scholarly books and was proud of their achievements. I had examined my own gifts, however, and decided that they could be better used at writing books for people who do not belong to the guild of scholars.

One of my colleagues—a critic whom I respect more than most—told me that my decision to quit the high ground of scholarship was a shame. In my shame-based years, his criticism would have made me feel very heavy. But more grace-based, I discovered I could take it lightly. I said to myself, "What you think of what I am doing matters some to me. But not much. I will not be shamed by your criticism."

Paul had still another critic—himself. His attitude toward his own criticism was the same as his attitude toward that of the critics outside: "I do not even take my criticisms of myself very seriously." By which he meant that when he faulted himself for something he did, he did not feel shame for what he was.

The secret? It comes in Paul's punch line: "The only thing that really matters is what the Lord thinks of me."

The Lord? The one with eyes that see everything? The nosy spy? The one Nietzsche declared a public nuisance? Yes, the Lord is my judge.

The Lord is the judge who accepts me by grace no matter how unacceptable any of my critics may judge me to be. The scare is gone and with it the shame—and with the shame, the heaviness.

I have been saying in this chapter that grace brings lightness to anyone heavy with shame. The lightness of grace does not lift all the sandbags that drag the spirit down. It lightens life by removing one very dead weight in particular—the weight of anxiety about being an unacceptable person. It extracts the internal threat of healthy shame. It gives us courage to track down the sources of unhealthy shame, see it for the undeserved pain it is, and take steps to purge our lives of it completely. It sets loose the lightest feeling of life; being accepted; totally, unreservedly accepted.

Twenty

The Return of Joy

In every real person the will for life is also the will for joy.

KARL BARTH

Grace is too unpredictable, too lavish, too delicious for us to stay sober about it. What can you do with such unchecked generosity but smack your lips, slosh it around your tongue, and savor it with joy?

I taste grace when a friend, for no reason at all, tells me that she loves me. I see it when my left leg goes where I tell it to go. I feel it when I take a deep breath of smog-free air. I savor it when the woman I have loved for forty years murmurs, strokes me, and asks me to move over to my side of the bed and give her some room to curl up beside me. I sense it as I wonder at the improbable oddity that all these thinking minds and feeling hearts and talking tongues should walk about on two legs, bustling around me on this one little globe in an immense universe that is itself floating among a trillion (apparently) lifeless universes.

I savor it most happily when I accept the fact that I am accepted as I am, with my ogres, my demons, and my angels, my blundered past, my frail virtues, all mixed together, undeserving and yet worthy at the same time, accepted by the Maker and Keeper of the universe.

Which brings me to my present point: the feeling called joy is the ultimate alternative to the feeling of shame. Joy, not shame, is our destiny. We know, don't we, by a kind of intuition, what joy is. Is it not the ecstasy of gratitude? Not cheerfulness, not humor, not drugged highs, but plain and simple thankfulness, deeply felt, down to the bone: is this not what joy is?

Joy usually seizes us when bad things suddenly turn good. My son calls after being flat abed for three months of horrible back pain and then suffering the soul pain of his one true love lost. He calls, I say, and tells me that he has received a promotion he badly wanted but did not dare expect. I finish a chapter I could not for weeks get right. My little girl has been lost for three hours, and I get a phone call from someone a few blocks down who tells me she is watching the television in her living room. The doctor calls to say that the tumor on my wife's left breast is benign.

But joy comes sometimes when the tumor is not benign and we do not get things right. It comes when we lose what we most desired and discover what we most needed. For me, as deep a joy as I can remember came while I mourned because I lost a new born child I wanted more than anyone should want anything on this earth. I cannot account for joy's odd invasion of a grief I intended to hoard against time's way of softening our sorrows. I only know that it came on me when I least wanted to feel it, came as a surge of hope that life can be good to live in spite of its badness, that it is all a gift—my wife, my friends, my children, my work, my loves, my desires—all together a fantastic gift. Oh, it flickered on and off, on for an instant here and a moment there, then an hour or two, and then off again. But it did come, and it keeps turning up every now and then when I think it must have left for good.

There is no right time for joy. The time our heart breaks may be the only time we have for it today. Joy does not repair the break; joy gets in between the splinters.

Joy comes, too, when a person looks back on her life, remembers how she finally owned the unpromising raw material she was given for the building of it, recalls her failures to build as well as she might have out of the materials she had, and finally one day makes peace both with what she was given and what she did with it, makes the peace that comes when one accepts the reality that she, with the whole of her life, is wholly and gladly accepted in the grace of God.

I sometimes wish I could make the peaks of joy last as long as the flatness. I want to catch the quick flushes of elation and stretch them over all my moments, all my life. However, joy seems to be an occasional thing.

One thing is sure: we feel the joy when it comes only if we are primed for it.

We cannot create joy. We certainly do not become joyful because somebody tells us we should. There is no computer program for joy. But if we cannot turn it on, we can certainly refuse to let it in.

We close the door to joy by letting certain myths about joy corrupt our sense of when and how we qualify for it. To keep ourselves open for joy, we need to make a myth check every now and then to see whether the myths we live by are robbing us of gratitude.

I am going to run through a few myths, six of them, actually, that have from time to time closed my consciousness to joy. I am going to counter each myth with a fact that has from time to time reopened it. You can check them out; maybe you will add one or two myths of your own.

> Myth: If you want joy, you have to earn it.
> Fact: If you have to earn joy, you will never get it.

This myth ruins some people's lives. Every time a little joy percolates into their feelings, they are jolted by a message from their long-departed mother or father that they do not deserve whatever it is they feel joyful about, and their joy drops dead on the spot.

The fact is that we never earn the gifts that surprise us with joy. Go back to basics: joy is gratitude. We feel gratitude only for gifts, and gifts are things we get but did not earn. But remember: a gift is not a gift simply because you got it for nothing. People can buy you by giving you things for nothing. A real gift never puts the receiver in debt. A real gift is only to enjoy.

The trick is to remember that we are worthy of gifts even though we do not deserve them. If we are made to feel unworthy of them, gifts shame us. But grace-based people know and feel that they are worthy of gifts that they could never earn or ever deserve.

Myth: When the chips are down, we get what we pay for.
Fact: When the chips are down, we get what we cannot pay for.

The fact is that I paid nothing for the breath I am taking at this moment. Or the mysterious energy that has kept my heart pumping ten million times without missing a beat. I did not pay a cent for the time I have on my hands. Or the touch of that woman's soft finger on the back of my hand. Not a penny for Mozart.

Most of all, I paid nothing for the grace that moves God to accept me and assure me that nothing that he knows about me will get him to stop accepting me—nothing I do or nothing I fail to be will even tempt him to hold back his grace and give me only what I deserve.

Myth: For joy to come, something unusual needs to happen.
Fact: The most unusual things happen in the usual things that usually happen.

I fancied I came home one night and said to Doris, "An amazing thing happened to me today."

I fancied she suspected a trick, but she answered me anyway: "Oh? Tell me about it."

"I told my left leg to move, and it did."

"That's amazing?"

That *is* amazing. Nobody has ever explained how a notion in our heads becomes a motion in our bodies. The link between a thought and an action is one of life's extraordinary commonplaces.

My leg made an exception once, ten minutes before I was to speak to an auditorium full of students at Seattle Pacific University. I was in the bathroom; I had just pulled up my trousers and told my leg to make its move toward the auditorium. My leg had other notions. It decided to stay put this time. What? Stay put? Has the world come unscrewed?

But wait. How come my left leg usually moves when I tell it to move? One reason the body does what the brain tells it to do is that the blood flowing toward our heads is usually precisely the right constituency: thick enough not to hemorrhage and thin enough not to clot somewhere in the brain. So most of the time we do not suffer strokes. But how does it usually pull it off? Incomprehensible! Enough to send us into a frenzy of joy every time we move our toes.

> Myth: Virtue is its own reward.
> Fact: Only joy is its own reward.

The only good thing about virtue is that it helps make life better for other people. Being of some earthly good to other people is the only good reason for being a good person. Anybody who wants virtue for its own sake is in for more shame than joy.

People who make a fuss about their virtue are forever trying to prove to themselves that they will never have reason to be ashamed of themselves. But they are never sure. This is why they work so hard at it and why they never really enjoy the virtue they have. It is not a means to an end.

Only joy is its own reward. It has no point and no purpose beyond itself. It is, however, the point and purpose of everything else. You never have to justify joy on grounds that it will help you sell more insurance or make you a better parent. If anyone asks us why we want joy in our lives, we should tell them, "Just because we enjoy it."

> Myth: If something is wrong, it is my job to fix it.
> Fact: Only God has the whole world in his hands.

If there is anything going wrong around them, shame-based people feel that they must fix it. They may not feel responsible for holes in the ozone layer or the destruction of the rain forests. But if they are parents and their grown children are in pain, they feel that it is up to them to heal it.

A wise woman once told me that I did not trust my children. I asked her to explain. "You don't trust them to suffer," she said. She was right. I have done some suffering and survived, but I do not trust my kids to cope with their own suffering. So if God does not prevent them from suffering, I feel that it is my job to do it. And when I cannot fix it, my joy leaves by the back door of my spirit.

Myth: We feel joy when our world is working right.
Fact: Our world never works right.

Every silver lining has a cloud. Cloudless joy comes when everything is right, when cancer never strikes and swords have become plowshares, when all children dance safely in their streets, and all tears are wiped away. When Shalom comes, then joy will have no clouds. But between now and then, joy comes between the clouds.

If all must be right with the world before I may have a fling with joy, I shall be somber forever.

The truth is that if we refuse to feel joy until every problem of the world is solved, every stomach full, every person housed, all violence stopped, we will have no joy this side of the New Earth. Joy in a world that does not work right must be a generous joy. Joy is always, always in spite of the fact that the whole world is groaning while it waits for its redemption.

These, then, are some of the joy-killing myths I have too much lived by. You have your own. Whatever myths we live by, we need to keep a check on them; they can close the door to joy and cause us to miss the point of living.

To give ourselves a fair chance at joy, we need now and then to stop the mythical, shame-encouraging world we live in, get off, and step into the real world of grace.

A World

Where unhealthy shame is obsolete.
Where healthy shame has lost its sting.
Where we know we are of great worth when we
    accept the grace we do not deserve.
Where bad choices of the past do not determine
    our worth today or forfeit our hopes
    for tomorrow.

Where we dare to feel guilty when guilty we are,
    for we know our guilt can be forgiven.
Where we celebrate our imperfections.
Where we can feel silly without feeling shame.
Where grace gives us reason to be proud
    of ourselves.
Where the lightness of grace lifts the heaviness
    of shame.
Where joy is the whole point.

Postscript:
A Faith for the Lighter Life

My friends, we will not go again or ape an ancient rage,
Or stretch the folly of our youth to be the shame of age,
For there is good news yet to hear and fine things to be seen,
Before we go to Paradise by way of Kensal Green.

G. K. CHESTERTON

I close with a personal statement that sums up most of what I have said about grace and the healing of shame. It is my way of staking out a claim for myself on grace.

Call it my commitment to faith. A faith for shame-free life, grace-based life, lighter life. I do not claim to live up to my faith, not yet, not consistently. I am still learning to live with grace instead of with shame, but it is the faith I want to live by, the faith I intend to live by. I hope that you will stake your own claim, in your own words, on the lighter life of grace. Whatever you do, however, here is my statement, my faith, and with it I close the book.

I believe that the only self I need to measure up to is the self my Maker meant me to be.

I believe that I am accepted by the grace of God without regard to my deserving.

I believe that I am accepted along with my shadows and the mix of good and bad I breed in them.

I believe that I am worthy to be accepted.

I believe that grace has set me free to accept myself totally, and without conditions, though I do not approve of everything I accept.

I believe that nothing I deserve to be ashamed of will ever make me unacceptable to God.

I believe that I can forgive anyone who has ever infected me with shame I do not deserve.

I believe that I may forgive myself for anything that I have ever done to shame myself or another person.

I am gratefully proud of being who I am and what I shall be.

I believe that the grace of God heals the shame I do not deserve and heals the shame I do.

I believe that grace is the best thing in the world.

For Further Reading

*Here are a few books that were
helpful to me in preparing to write this book.*

Au, Wilkie. *By Way of the Heart.* New York: Paulist Press, 1989.

Becker, Ernest. *Escape from Evil.* New York: Free Press, 1975.

Bonhoeffer, Dietrich. *Ethics.* New York: Macmillan, 1955.

Bradshaw, John. *Healing the Shame That Binds You.* Deerfield Beach,
	Florida: Health Communications, 1988.

Camus, Albert. *The Fall.* New York: Vintage Books, 1956.

Dostoyevski, Fyodor. *The Idiot.* London: Dent & Son, 1914.

Gaylin, Willard. *Feelings.* New York: Ballantine, 1974.

Groeschel, Benedict. *Spiritual Passages.* New York: Crossroad, 1988.

John of the Cross. *Selected Writings.* New York: Paulist Press, 1987.

Johnson, Robert A. *Owning Your Own Shadow.* San Francisco: HarperSan-
	Francisco, 1991.

Kaufman, Gershen. *The Psychology of Shame.* Cambridge: Schenkman,
	1989.

Kaufman, Gershen. *Shame, the Power of Caring.* Cambridge: Schenkman,
	1990.

Lewis, Helen Block. *Shame and Guilt in Neurosis.* New York: International
	Universities Press, 1974.

Lewis, Michael. *Shame, the Exposed Self.* New York: Free Press, 1992.

Nathanson, D. L., ed. *The Many Faces of Shame.* New York: Guilford
	Press, 1987.

Niebuhr, Reinhold. *The Nature and Destiny of Man.* New York: Macmil-
	lan, 1964.

Piers, G., and M. B. Singer. *Shame and Guilt.* New York: Norton, 1953.

Sample, Albert Race. *Racehoss: Big Emma's Boy.* Austin, Texas: Eakin Press,
	1984.

Sartre, Jean Paul. *Being and Nothingness*. New York: Washington Square
    Press, 1966 (original, 1943).
Schneider, Carl. *Shame, Exposure, and Privacy*. Boston: Beacon Press, 1977.
Tournier, Paul. *Guilt and Grace*. New York: Harper & Row, 1962.
Vorst, Judith. *Necessary Losses*. New York: Simon & Schuster, 1989.

Notes

CHAPTER 6: SPIRITUAL SHAME: THE PRICE WE PAY TO SEE GOD?

1. Psalm 139:1–3.
2. Job 7:19, 20.
3. Isaiah 6:5.

CHAPTER 7: SOCIAL SHAME: THE PAIN OF REJECTION

1. Job 17:6.
2. John 1:11.
3. Hebrews 12:2.
4. Luke 6:22.
5. Jeremiah 6:15.

CHAPTER 13: THE BEGINNING OF OUR HEALING

1. Published as *Racehoss: Big Emma's Boy* (Austin, Texas: Eakin Press, 1984).

CHAPTER 18: ACCEPTING OURSELVES

1. Etty kept a diary that was published four decades after her death under the title *An Interrupted Life* (New York: Pocket Books, 1985).
2. 2 Corinthians 1:14.

CHAPTER 19: LIVING LIFE LIGHTLY

1. Galatians 2:20.
2. 1 Corinthians 4:2–4.